The Scott and Laurie Oki Series
in Asian American Studies

Storied Lives

Japanese
American
Students and
World War II

Gary Y. Okihiro

WITH A CONTRIBUTION BY

Leslie A. Ito

UNIVERSITY OF WASHINGTON PRESS
SEATTLE AND LONDON

To the nisei students
and their collaborators in resistance

This book is published with the assistance of a grant from the Scott and Laurie Oki Endowed Fund for the publication of Asian American Studies, established through the generosity of Scott and Laurie Oki.

LIBRARY OF CONGRESS CATALOGING-IN-PUBLICATION DATA

Okihiro, Gary Y. , 1945–
    Storied lives : Japanese American students and World War II / Gary Y. Okihiro ; with a contribution by Leslie A. Ito.
        p.   cm. — (The Scott and Laurie Oki series in Asian American studies)
    Includes bibliographical references and index.
    ISBN 0-295-97764-7 (cloth : alk. paper). — ISBN 0-295-97796-5 (pbk. : alk. paper)
        1. World War, 1939–1945 — Japanese Americans.   2. Japanese American college students — Social conditions.   3. Japanese American college students — Economic conditions.   4. Racism — United States — History — 20th century.   5. United States — Race relations.   1. Ito, Leslie A.   II. Title.   III. Series.
    D753.8.O38   1999   98–51100
    940.53'089'956073 — dc21   CIP

The paper used in this publication is acid-free and recycled from 10 percent post-consumer and at least 50 percent pre-consumer waste. It meets the minimum requirements of American National Standard for Information Sciences-Permanence of paper for Printed Library Materials, ANSI Z39.48-1984. ♻ ♾

CONTENTS

ACKNOWLEDGMENTS

Kesaya E. Noda first approached me to undertake this book project, and from the beginning Lafayette Noda and Nobu K. Hibino have helped me in my work. My associate in this venture, Leslie A. Ito, wrote a marvelous undergraduate honors thesis on this subject that inspired me, and my research assistant and graduate student, Mary Ting Yi Lui, sent hundreds of letters to colleges and universities and organized their responses. I am grateful to the scores of archivists and alumni office staff members, not all named in this book, who rendered invaluable and generous assistance in searching their records and sending me whatever information they could find on nisei students at their institutions. Former student relocation staff members and nisei students graciously admitted me into their lives and allowed me to record their reminiscences. Thomas R. Bodine and Lafayette Noda commented on the draft manuscript that became this book, along with the two perceptive, though anonymous, readers chosen by the University of Washington Press. This account is clearer and more accurate as a result. Having now published three books with the University of Washington Press, I must mention with gratitude the support given to me (and the field of Asian American Studies generally) by the Press and especially its associate director and editor-in-chief, Naomi B. Pascal. Finally, Cornell University and the Japanese American National Museum provided me with the funds to carry out this research, which took me across the country. All of the materials gathered for this project are on deposit at the Japanese American National Museum in Los Angeles. Like the subjects of this study, I am indebted to the many who have helped me.

PREFACE

I must confess that I resisted the idea of this slender text, *Storied Lives: Japanese American Students and World War II*. When first asked by Kesaya E. Noda to write yet another history of the wartime experience of Japanese Americans, I refused the suggestion. Not another book on a much-discussed subject, I thought to myself as I looked out the window to the sleepy Charles River below in Cambridge, Massachusetts. I was at the time concerned about the continued emphasis of Asian American Studies on Chinese and Japanese Americans and subject matters like the transcontinental railroad and wartime concentration camps. I agreed with Elaine Kim's ringing call for the field to move "beyond railroads and internment," and thought that I had done my part in promoting those centrisms that have advanced but also retarded the field's development. And I loathed the prospect of further complicity in a topic that has, I must say, become an industry of sorts motivated by disagreeable political and economic interests for their own ends. Although hugely important, America's wartime concentration camps was not the entirety of Japanese, much less Asian, American history.

So my initial impulse was to decline Noda's proposal. I had other commitments, I demurred, and was hopelessly behind in my work. But she persisted and told me about the Nisei Student Relocation Commemorative Fund, described by Leslie A. Ito in this book's afterword, and I was intrigued and moved by the story of how a group of former nisei college students had joined together decades later to help another group of students, Southeast Asian refugees, who were like them victims of war. I thought the deed amazing and wonderful.

My enthusiasm for the subject matter warmed when archivists and staff members from dozens of institutions offered their assistance in response to my query for help. Many expressed great interest in this project, and spent innumerable hours searching through their holdings and photocopying items for me. Those efforts saved me enormous amounts of time and resources that would have been required for visits to campuses scattered across the country. They also provided me with insights into nisei student life and the campus cultures peculiar to their institutions during the World War II years.

But what truly fired my imagination were the student records themselves and the correspondence between nisei students and their collaborators in resistance to the racism of the concentration camps. Reading them, bundles of them, I was swept away by the individual circumstances of each nisei correspondent and by the equally personal responses of staff members of the various student relocation groups. I had expected to find the form letters typical of bureaucracies because of the masses of correspondence generated by the project and because of the laborious process of typing without the benefit of word-processing and photocopying. Manual typewriters are now relics of the past, but I well remember the frustrations of typing multiple copies using carbon paper. I was astonished to find stacks of letters for each student, held in folders, written as if the correspondents were intimate friends. I was confounded and deeply affected, especially by the letters lovingly written by Trudy King, Tom Bodine, and Kay Yamashita.

Before that discovery, I was skeptical of the entire program of nisei student relocation and of Whites who participated in the project. I knew too well the deeds of other Whites on behalf of their Asian American wards. Their work of charity often carried the added baggage of paternalism or maternalism, termed "white racist love" by Asian American writers,[1] that was frequently folded within the envelope of Christian missions and social uplift. Donaldina Cameron and her cohort at the Mission Home on Sacramento Street in San Francisco's Chinatown about the turn of the century might have "rescued" dozens of Chinese women and girls from the clutches of prostitution, but they also held some of their charges against their will, sought to transform their culture, promoted their own social standing among Whites, and believed in their moral and cultural superiority.[2] Antisexism (and antiracism) might have racist (and sexist) purposes and ends. Deeds can have multiple dimensions, and appearances can deceive.

Likewise, the War Relocation Authority's objectives of relocation and assimilation bore the stench of white racism. Couched as benevolence, those colonizing acts of cultural (if not physical) erasure identified Japanese Americans as "the problem" and consequently determined to absorb them into the white mainstream. White racism, the argument went, was caused by Japanese Americans: they looked like the enemy, shared the religion, food, language, and behavior of the enemy, and lived in concentrations called Little Tokyos along the West Coast. That very visibility, the social engineers maintained, prompted an instinctual recoiling and hostility by Whites. Thus they planned the dispersion of Japanese Americans—their "relocation" and "education"—to "Americanize" them or to get them to assimilate and adopt white cultural identities. Japanese Americans were taught to be like Whites, and some overeager Japanese American pupils measured their success even after the war by "outwhiting the Whites."[3]

The stereotype, in truth, of the nisei generation as a whole is that of the assimilated superpatriot who was 110 percent American. The Japanese American Citizens League, founded by nisei in 1930, adopted its creed in 1940 to show, in part, the degree to which its members committed themselves to "the American way." "Because I believe in America," the creed concludes, " . . . I pledge myself to do honor to her at all times and in all places; to support her Constitution; to obey her laws; to respect the flag; to defend her against all enemies, foreign or domestic; to actively assume my duties and obligations as a citizen, cheerfully and without reservations whatsoever, in the hope that I may become a better American in a greater America."[4] Although seemingly following the pattern deemed "natural" for European immigrants of the first generation (old country) and second generation (new country), nisei (and indeed European) "Americanization" had to be engineered during the 1920s and 1930s in the public schools and in campaigns directed at targeted groups.[5] That special attention was necessary because those populations resisted wholesale assimilation and because ethnic pluralism, the Americanizers declared, threatened the Republic's presumed homogeneity and hence domestic tranquility. Those same assumptions and conclusions guided the wartime strategy of relocation.

"It would be good for the United States generally and I think it would be good from the standpoint of the Japanese-Americans themselves, to be scattered over a much wider area and not to be

bunched up in groups as they were along the Coast," declared Dillon
S. Myer, director of the War Relocation Authority, at a press conference in 1943. Relocation, he stated, would help solve "a serious racial
problem by having them scattered throughout the United States
instead of bunched up in three or four states."[6] Of course, the director spoke only a half-truth when he faulted Japanese Americans for
their prewar clustering in three or four western states, because concentration arose out of necessity as well as choice, depending on the
places that would allow them livelihoods and residence. Racism precluded their unabated social and physical mobility. And the "racial
problem" of which Myer spoke was not the "Japanese problem" but
the "white problem" insofar as racism emanated from Whites and not
from Japanese racial or cultural difference.

Relocation, thus, like the policies of American Indian removal,
trusteeship, and termination, was profoundly racist.[7] I was convinced of that, and accordingly believed the project of nisei student
relocation to have been a variant of "white racist love." But as I soon
learned from my research, the motivations and deeds of Whites who
labored in student relocation—as I show in the following pages—
were complex and at odds with the overarching aims of the War Relocation Authority, an agency to which the student relocation effort was
nonetheless closely tied. And my thinking about the subject of white
philanthropy and its many-sided and sometimes contrary faces
prompted me to reflect upon the meanings and manifestations of
racism and its counter, antiracism.

The definitions and deeds of white racism fill shelves, indeed entire
libraries. But rare, in contrast, are the books on white antiracism. Asian
American historiography attests to the veracity of that general obser-
vation. Race, of course, is the singular pivot upon which the field turns,
and the racialization of Asians in America is typically described and
analyzed through the lenses of the anti-Asian movement and anti-
Asianism. As I have proposed elsewhere,[8] the literature on Asian Americans began with cultural brokers, mainly Whites but also Asians, who
sought to translate the Asian "other" to white Americans for mutual
understanding and economic gain. Anti-Asianists offered another view
of Asians; and liberals, in turn, responded to the assertions of the anti-
Asianists. A final group, the Asian Americanists as I've called them,
wrote to create a sense of identity and community and a notion of

historical agency. But whatever the purpose or claim, writings on Asian Americans are largely distinguished by their racialized subject matter and emphasis on white racism and, to a lesser degree, Asian antiracism, as decisive in the formation of Asian racial subjectivities.

White antiracism must almost be intuited from the prodigious body of works on white racism. As oppositional pairs, racism and antiracism hinge upon each other. One is what the other is not. If racism sought exclusion, thus antiracism sought inclusion. Or if racism denied a people their culture, then antiracism worked to secure that culture. Clearly, however, there are complications to those binaries. Inclusion, for example, may be fundamentally racist if it means the forced absorption or assimilation of a group, and assertions of ethnicity or culture can be emphatically racist if they create exclusive islands of ethnic authority and privilege. Antiracism, like racism, must be situated in time and place—historicized—in order to see it in its fullness and true light. Despite criticism, universities and colleges during the war admitted nisei students, thus an antiracist act; but they sometimes placed limits on the numbers they would accept, a racist act. The Relocation Council enabled nisei education, an antiracist act; but also advised nisei students to avoid clustering and impressed upon them the need to be model students—both racist suggestions. And yet, those determinations derived from a calculus of initiatives and constraints. Society's racism, institutions concluded, prevented them from accepting large numbers of nisei students; and racism, the Council reasoned, required a demonstration by nisei of their assimilability, excellence, and worth. Racism and antiracism alike are contingent and slippery categories.

A final word about this book. Its title evokes both the medium through which I recall this history—stories—and the immensity of the deeds of my subjects, white and Japanese American, whose seemingly uneventful lives were truly storied. And although its subtitle is generous, this work is limited to a discussion of Japanese American college students. Those interested in the elementary and secondary years might want to read Thomas James's account.[9] Others who are seeking an institutional history of the National Japanese American Student Relocation Council should consult the commissioned study by Robert W. O'Brien.[10] I determined early on that this book, unlike O'Brien's, would be devoted to the nisei students and those individuals who helped them. Accordingly, I surveyed the colleges and universities the nisei attended, collected oral histories from twenty-seven nisei students and student relocation staff members, and worked my way through the pertinent records and papers held at Stanford's Hoover Institution; but I neglected the archives and papers of the War Relocation Authority, American Friends Service Committee, YWCA and YMCA, and churches and foundations, all of which played key roles in the project of student relocation. And I relied heavily upon the Council's nisei student records, and thus regretted deeply the loss of nine out of ten of those files from the Records of the National Japanese American Student Relocation Council, 1942–1946, because Hoover's archivist decided they were too bulky for historical preservation and threw them away.[11]

Despite their focus on the seemingly narrow topic of nisei student relocation, those collective records shed new and important light on the broader contexts of war and society, Japanese American history, America's concentration camps, and life outside of the camps. Student letters, for instance, detail family circumstances before and after the mass removals and detentions, along with conditions within and outside the assembly centers and concentration camps. And the strategies deployed by Japanese Americans to oppose racism and sexism, including the use of and dependence upon Whites and investments in education, and the counsel urged by Whites for the nisei to pose as model students and loyal Americans, paved the way for the postwar stereotype of the model minority—exemplary citizens and whiz kids. That image was enhanced by the Council's understandable though regrettable touting of nisei "success stories" of student overachievers to blunt criticism of the program and gain vital financial support for the effort. Because of my concern over the model minority stereotype and its current prevalence and insidiousness (I am here thinking about its logic deployed in rolling back affirmative action in college admissions), I have not privileged the few, who compiled exceptional student records and also postgraduate careers, at the expense of the many, whose achievements were less stellar and "ordinary." Most, I believe, were emphatically extraordinary.

Storied Lives

Japanese
American
Students and
World War II

An
Uneventful
Life

THE STORY IS SKETCHY, but the record is there, housed in boxes among the yellowing papers deposited at an archive in California. "On the morning of April sixteenth 1924 I was born on this earth in the quiet town of Alameda," the autobiography of this American began. "I grew up in a normal life, not handicapped by any physical injuries or illness. My life till twelve years of age was as uneventful as that of any other child."

His life changed, recalled Roy Nakata, the writer, when he joined the Boy Scouts at the age of twelve, and for the next two years went camping with the troop to nearby places and, most memorably, Yosemite National Park. "Here for two weeks, I spent the most enjoyable time I have ever had," he remembered. "Fishing, cooking outdoors, hiking, and visiting the many beautiful spots that surrounded our camp was my daily routine."

Those Boy Scout outings, Nakata wrote, were a turning point in his "uneventful" life. "After my return from this [Yosemite] trip," he observed, "my mother told me how surprised she was in the way a simple camping trip could affect one so. According to her, the two things I definitely gained from this trip were a milder disposition, and a feeling of independence in my actions."

But this brief autobiography takes another turn. In Nakata's words: "there is always a dark side to every happy side in life, so it was with our family." The event was the completion of the Bay Bridge that connected Berkeley with San Francisco. With the bridge came a decline in ferry passengers, and Nakata's father, a ferryman for eigh-teen years, was laid off. In search of employment, the senior Nakata moved his family across the bay from Alameda to Los Altos.

Nakata was then in his first year at Alameda High School, and the transfer to the high school in Mountain View, the nearest one to Los Altos, was dislocating. "Because of my transfer," he admitted, "my efforts ought to have been doubled in a readjustment to a new school; but instead, I continued at my former pace, so that my grades sharply dropped." His parents, hoping to reverse that slide, moved the fam-ily to Palo Alto, where the high school had a reputation for very high academic standards. "Thinking of my education more than anything else," he wrote, "my parents, my sister and myself, moved to Palo Alto."

The move and his family's sacrifice sobered him, and Nakata applied himself to his studies. But again, external forces were to intervene in this family's drive for economic security. Japan's attack on Pearl Har-bor in 1941 and his government's decision to remove and confine all West Coast Japanese the following year threatened to end Nakata's education. "Now with my graduation almost in sight, this terrible war has made it necessary that we, Americans of Japanese ancestry, be evacuated from the coast states," Nakata wrote in the spring of 1942. All he needed to complete high school was a required hygiene course, and his teacher, in expectation of his forced expulsion from his home and school, gave him extra work so he could fulfill the course requirements before the military closed the door on his education.

"As I, an American of Japanese ancestry, stand today on the threshhold [*sic*] of success or failure in life," Nakata resolved, "I have a definite plan to continue studying and try my humble part in serv-ing in the best possible manner this great land of America." That ambi-tion, he reported, was impelled by his parents' determination. "Instead of my being sent to an internment camp and wasting away what lit-tle knowledge I have gained thus far, as well as the much precious time," he wrote, "my parents tell me that they are willing to sacrifice all they have towards my education. It is my sincere hope that I be allowed the privilege of attending an institution of good name so that I may fulfill their dreams, and so that I may mold myself into a bet-ter American and do my part in building an even greater America."[1]

Roy Nakata's story, although incomplete and fragmented, tells a stirring tale of the human spirit amid despair and inhumanity. It involved not only a young man and his caring and supportive family, but a host of others whose deeds affected his life's tracings. These included President Franklin D. Roosevelt, whose Executive Order 9066 signed February 19, 1942, began the process of mass removal and detention of Japanese along the West Coast; Nakata's high school teachers and administrators, who facilitated his graduation in the face of an impending military order; and, unmentioned in this version of his autobiography, Alice Sinclair Dodge, the employer of Nakata's family.

Alice Sinclair Dodge was the daughter of a college professor in Worcester, Massachusetts. She married a minister, Rowland B. Dodge, in 1905 in Honolulu, and moved with him to Maui. There, until 1919, he was pastor of the Wailuku Union Church and headed all Congregationalist churches on the island. In 1924, the Dodges moved to Palo Alto, and there became the employers of the Nakata family when they moved from Los Altos to Palo Alto for the sake of Roy's education.

"Roy Nakata's father and mother have both helped in our home at different times for several years," Mrs. Dodge explained in a letter to the dean of Oberlin College in Ohio. "We came to respect them and appreciate their difficulties and they turned to us to ask what they could do to assure Roy of a good education. They had decided since they were forced to leave California for a Relocation Camp that this was the time to use all the family savings,—a very little over $2000.—, for Roy's education." She took up the Nakatas' appeal for help, and, despite "all sorts of difficulties to overcome," Roy was admitted to and allowed to attend Oberlin College in the fall of 1942 "through our personal efforts. . . ."[2]

Those "personal efforts" must have been considerable. Although he apparently completed the hygiene course and managed to graduate from Palo Alto High School, Roy Nakata was picked up by the military's sweep of the West Coast. Before leaving for the detention camps, however, his parents deposited their "family savings" into a bank under Mrs. Dodge's name for her disposition, because the government had frozen the banking assets of first-generation Japanese in December 1941. Roy Nakata thus spent the summer of 1942 with his family in Santa Anita Assembly Center in southern California, "waiting and hoping and praying," in Mrs. Dodge's words.

Nakata's letters to Alice Sinclair Dodge from Santa Anita shed some light on how the government's actions affected his family. "Home" for the Nakatas at Santa Anita was a converted horse stall. Santa Anita, like Tanforan in northern California, was a race track that had been hastily transformed into an "assembly center" for the evicted Japanese Americans. Horse stalls, their interiors of rough boards, protruding nails, and spider webs whitewashed over but still reeking of manure, were some of the first "barracks" for the government's keep. Besides suffering those indignities, Nakata's family had to endure physical discomfort. "The temperature here is a little too uncomfortable for taking a nap to compensate for my sleepiness," Nakata explained. "You see, the temperature in the horse stall barracks reach[es] over 103 degrees in the afternoon."

The family thankfully moved from the horse stall in July, Nakata noted, to a barracks "apartment" constructed, of wood and "covered with thin tar paper." And "rough though it may be," he wrote it had wooden floors and never had housed a horse, and for that "we are very grateful and thankful." Windows on both ends allowed for a cross-draft, and, as a consequence, Nakata observed, "these rooms are considerably cooler than the units of the horse stall barracks."

Mrs. Dodge sent the Nakatas copies of *Reader's Digest,* and, because she was in northern California, wrote to a friend in Claremont in southern California asking her to visit and possibly attend to the Nakatas at Santa Anita. The friend, however, was out of town at the time, and so wrote to her friend, who passed the request on to her friend, Katherine Fanning, who visited the Nakatas in the "assembly center," bringing "some things that we [the Nakatas] had ordered." Fanning, a stranger to the Nakatas, extended her hand of kindness in their time of great need.

Recognizing his family's indebtedness to Mrs. Dodge, Nakata expressed his gratitude in a letter to her. "Mrs. Dodge, please do not worry so kindly for us," he wrote somewhat awkwardly but with undisguised feeling. "Haven't you done so much already that we know of no way to thank you? We really do appreciate all your kindness from the bottoms of our hearts but certainly this is too much. Thank you ever and ever for all your sincere kindness." With nothing to offer her, Nakata sent her "a piece of carving I did for you in my spare time"— a heart carved from a wood knot. "Though it is nothing very good,

I made it from a piece of pine knot that I found," he wrote. "It has been polished only by rubbing with a piece of soft cloth." He included a drawing in his letter with the approximate location of the heart-figure on the knot, showing the direction of the grains on the whole knot and carving, "the pointed end of the heart being the center of the knot," he explained in loving detail and with some precision.[3]

Roy Nakata's letter, besides revealing personal experiences and feelings, also offered observations of life in the Santa Anita camp. The high school was dissolved, he reported in June 1942, and junior high school was the highest level attainable. The camp administrators, had concluded that they would draft "all boys of sixteen years of age or over" to work making camouflage nets for the military. "Perhaps I did not tell you that the boys here are forced, especially the late arrivals, to work by indirect threats on the camoflage [*sic*] project," confided Nakata. Threatened with transfer to the Poston concentration camp at Parker Dam, Arizona, "a hot, dry wasteland, I hear," or with being put on a "black-list and be discriminated about the camp," the youth were encouraged to make camouflage nets forty hours each week for eight dollars a month.[4]

Isolated in a government detention camp, Roy Nakata had to rely on the kindness of his family's patron, Alice Sinclair Dodge. To assure Nakata "a good education," she had several hurdles to overcome. She had to locate a college or university that would accept her charge at a time when administrators commonly refused to admit Japanese American students, simply on the basis of their "race." The application process involved coordinating letters of recommendation from Nakata's high school teachers, seeing that his high school grade transcripts were sent, and having him fill out the application form and write his college essay. Even after his application was accepted, in order to be released from the detention camp, Nakata, with Mrs. Dodge's assistance, had to cope with the government bureaucracy that required proof of admission and financial solvency along with attestations of his good character.

Nakata's dependence on Mrs. Dodge continued while he was a student at Oberlin College. Writing on December 6, 1942, and with the approach of the Christmas holidays, Nakata told her of his "sudden need." "I have with me about $1.50 now," he informed her. "This is what I have left over from the sum of the money you sent me and the money I had on myself when I left Santa Anita." His books for the fall term, he reported, cost $12.02, including $3.09 for a mathematics textbook, $4.12 for a dictionary, $1.18 for *The Iliad*, $1.65 for a German book, and $1.03 for a classical dictionary. Tuition was $150; board, $120; and $13.53 was required for the student activity fee. He bought three pairs of socks, three shirts, a sweater, gloves and mufflers, a pair of shoes, and a gymnastic outfit, along with a freshman cap that cost 50 cents. He joined the mathematics club and cosmopolitan club with dues of 25 and 50 cents, bought shoe polish for 16 cents, paid $2.95 for shower slippers, went to two movies for 80 cents, bought 40 cents worth of candy, and had six haircuts. His expenditures for the term totaled $362.28, which didn't include his expenses "for food on the train during my trip and the sport coat that I had to buy in Sacramento during the 5 hour wait there." "As I figure," he concluded from his detailed accounting, "a check for about $35.00 would be greatly appreciated," and added, "I am sorry that I delayed so long before telling you of my sudden need."[5]

In truth, the correspondence between Roy Nakata and Alice Sinclair Dodge reveals much of importance about the Japanese American, and Asian American, experience. The autobiography of this "uneventful" life, archived and preserved for future generations, was rendered significant by the global winds that shaped the career of this American and by historians equally attentive to the deeds of society's elites as well as its masses. Roy Nakata's "sudden need" was prompted by the events of World War II, specifically by the action of his government in evicting and detaining all of the West Coast's Japanese Americans.

World War II, to be sure, exacted a heavy toll on scores of Americans, but also provided unprecedented opportunities for many others. Most Japanese Americans, like other American minorities and women, generally shared in the war's deficits but few of its gains.[6] Insofar as they were rendered dependent by their government's detention program, Japanese Americans frequently had to rely on the generosity of others. As recalled by Alice Sinclair Dodge, the Nakatas "turned to us" during "their difficulties." The theme of interaction between Whites and Asians is clearly one of the foundations of Asian American history. But this particular interaction goes against the grain of most accounts of the Japanese American experience during the

World War II period—accounts that detail the prewar racism of white Americans marshaled into an anti-Japanese movement that culminated with the concentration camps. Indeed, white racism has become a given, almost a truism, in the historical literature, but a stereotype nonetheless of an undifferentiated majority. Although the subject of this book—nisei college students during World War II—owes much of its character to the interventions of white racism, it also testifies to the presence and strength of white antiracism. The deeds of Alice Sinclair Dodge and many others like her must not go unrecognized.

Those acts of antiracism were complemented by the initiatives taken and forged by Japanese Americans who were determined to chart their own lives despite the encircling barbed wire fence of the concentration camps. Roy Nakata's parents, according to his account, were willing to sacrifice all they had toward his education—their family savings of just over $2,000. That investment, they must have believed, would allow their son to achieve some measure of the American promise of equal opportunity and thereby figuratively unlock the restrictive gates of the racist concentration camps.

Those twin achievements of antiracism, by Japanese Americans and their white allies, came at a crucial time in the development of Japanese America. The nisei, or second generation, came of age during the 1930s and 1940s. As Roy Nakata described it in his college application essay, he stood on "the threshhold [*sic*] of success or failure in life." Perhaps he overstated his prospects, but he assuredly stood at a major crossroad. Of the 110,000 Japanese Americans on the West Coast in 1941, about 70,000 were nisei, and of those about 3,300 were in colleges and universities, mainly in a few large public universities in California. During the war, over 5,500 left the concentration camps for college. Their postsecondary education was not only important for those young women and men as individuals and members of families, but also for the well-being of the wider collective, the Japanese American community.

Reduced to its essentials and in retrospect, this story might be read by some as an affirmation of the "model minority" stereotype that became commonplace during the 1980s and 1990s—the supposed emphasis by Asians on family and education for upward mobility and assimilation into American life. The 1980s and 1990s version had its beginnings in the World War II removal and detention of Japanese

Americans, creating the baseline for their remarkable ascent. "California's Amazing Japanese" the *Saturday Evening Post* of April 30, 1955, declared less than a decade after the doors closed at the last concentration camp, were the "major beneficiaries of the long and savage war between Japan and the United States." The author turned the injustice upon its head: "Japanese residents of California have lifted themselves higher in a few postwar years than they had done in the preceding half century. And agitation against them has been almost silenced."[7]

But like all stereotypes, the notion of the model minority is a caricature of a messier and more complex reality.[8] World War II was not an unmitigated "blessing in disguise" for Japanese Americans: educational achievement alone failed to ensure economic and social equality, much less "success," and Asian Americans are not without their needs and shortcomings. In contrast to generalizing and homogenizing stereotypes, whether they refer to "amazing Japanese" or racist Whites, the core of the story recounted in this book is about individuals, both Japanese and white Americans, who were constrained but not bound by circumstances and who sometimes conformed to external impositions and at other times resisted them. It is also a complicated story, wanting in unqualified heroes and villains, that began centuries before Roy Nakata was born in the sleepy town of Alameda, California.

Perhaps the story's beginnings might be found in Europe's search for a passage to India, to the fabulous East, where spices, teas, silks, textiles, and porcelain could be had to enrich a merchant, a ship's captain, a company, a nation. Some, like Marco Polo during the thirteenth century, ventured across the vast landmasses of Europe and Asia to Cathay; others, like Christopher Columbus during the fifteenth century, sailed across the equally immense bodies of water "to the regions of India, to see the Princes there and the peoples and the lands, and to learn of their disposition, and of everything," in the admiral's words.[9] America's "discovery" by Europeans, of course, was the result of that appetite for Asia's products.

It is interesting to note that an icon of America's freedom from British rule, the Boston Tea Party, had to do with one of Asia's goods — tea. Taxation without representation was the patriots' cry, but the importation of duty-free tea to the colonies by the British East India

Company in 1773 threatened not the masses but a class of America's merchants who couldn't compete with the Company's cheaper tea. The Asian trade figured prominently in both America's "discovery" and the founding of the United States. In 1784, the year after the last British troops embarked from New York's harbor and George Washington rode into the city at the head of the triumphant American forces, the *Empress of China,* loaded with New England ginseng, sailed from that same port for China. The business venture was underwritten, in part, by Robert Morris, a wealthy merchant and the "financier of the American Revolution," and when it returned just over a year later, the *Empress* yielded a satisfactory 25 to 30 percent profit to its investors. More important, for some of the Republic's leaders, it presaged a trade that heralded a severance of dependence upon Europe and national greatness.

America's overland advance to the Pacific Ocean was similarly motivated by the Asian trade and the hoped for global ascendancy that would result from that commerce. This is what Thomas Jefferson had in mind when, as president, he dispatched Meriwether Lewis and William Clark in 1803 to find a route to the Pacific "for the purposes of commerce." Although impractical at the time as an economic scheme, the expedition, wrote scholar Henry Nash Smith, "lay on the level of imagination; it was a drama, it was the enactment of a myth that embodied the future. It gave tangible substance to what had been merely an idea, and established the image of a highway across the continent so firmly in the minds of Americans that repeated failures could not shake it." Because when Lewis and Clark reached the shore of the Pacific in 1804, observed Smith, "they reactivated the oldest of all ideas associated with America—that of a passage to India."[10]

America's seizure of lands in the Southwest from Mexico in 1848 made it, indeed, a Pacific nation. Standing on California's shore, the Republic claimed the continent as its manifest destiny, and gazed upon the waters of the Pacific glimmering gold. Commodore Matthew C. Perry's "opening" of Japan in 1854 to Western commerce, and United States annexation of the Philippines and Hawaii in 1898, were chapters in the narratives of Europe's and America's quest for Asia's wealth.

Hawaii itself was "discovered" or more accurately placed on European maps by British Captain James Cook in 1778, when he bumped into the islands on his way to North America's western flank, searching for the fabled Northwest Passage that would allow direct access from Europe to Asia. Thereafter, Hawaii's harbors sheltered European and American ships involved in the Asian trade, and the islands supplied sandalwood, an aromatic tree used in incense, that was exchanged for Asia's products. Europeans and Americans also settled on Hawaiian shores, introducing diseases that decimated Hawaii's indigenous peoples, as well as ideologies of capitalism and Christianity that eventually supplanted, but did not extinguish, the prevailing social relations and systems of belief, and establishing sugar plantations that drew and employed scores of Hawaiian and imported laborers.

The kingdom's foreign minister, who was also a plantation owner, inquired of an American businessman in Japan: "Could any good agricultural laborers be obtained from Japan or its dependencies to serve like the Chinese, under contract for 6 or 8 years? If so, send me all the information you can and state at what cost per head they could be landed here; and if their wives and children could be induced to come with them." The year was 1865, and Hawaii was experiencing a labor shortage and sugar boom, because America's Civil War (1861–65) had disrupted the South's sugar production and the North's access to it. The query led to the recruitment of 141 Japanese men, 6 women, and 2 children, called the *gannenmono,* or "first year people" (so called because they migrated during the first year of the Meiji era), for Hawaii's sugar plantations in 1868.

Labor migration, such as that of the *gannenmono,* was a central feature of Euroamerican trade with Asia that included both goods and people. European plantations, established in the world's tropical zone, required laborers who were shipped from Africa and Asia to places like the Caribbean basin, including the U.S. South, and Hawaii. Those Asian indentured laborers prominently involved Asian Indian and Chinese "coolies" and Hawaii's Japanese contract workers. Likened to commodities, Asians were fetched to tend the master's fields of cane. Hawaii's planters, for example, routinely placed orders that included human beings along with other needed supplies (bonemeal, canvas, Japanese laborers, macaroni, and a "Chinaman") — or sometimes their lists were alphabetical (as in fertilizer and Filipinos).[11]

Japanese were also driven to America by conditions in Japan, such as when the Pacific Mail Company's *China* sailed into San Francisco Bay in 1869, about a year after the arrival of Hawaii's *gannenmono*, with a group of samurai, farmers and tradesmen, and four women. Sent by their displaced lord, Matsudaira Katamori, to explore the potential for a settlement, the pioneers left San Francisco, headed up the Sacramento River to Placerville, and established the Wakamatsu Tea and Silk Farm Colony on 600 acres of land. Like the *gannenmono*, this experiment failed and many returned to Japan; but some of them stayed, married local women, produced offspring, and constituted some of the earliest Japanese communities in Hawaii and the U.S. mainland.

Others followed, mainly men but also women and children, as migrant workers, students, businessmen, Buddhist missionaries, brothers, sons and daughters, and picture brides. Between 1885 and 1894, about 29,000 Japanese recruited by Robert Walker Irwin, Hawaiian consul general and special agent for immigration, made the crossing to Hawaii as government-contract migrants. Approximately 125,000 more went to the islands as "free migrants" from 1894 to 1908, when the Gentlemen's Agreement between Japan and the U.S. halted the further migration of male laborers. Women were a mere 9 percent of Hawaii's Japanese in 1890, increased to 22 percent in 1900, 31 percent in 1910, and 41 percent in 1920. About 27,440 Japanese migrated to the U.S. mainland between 1891 and 1900, and 42,457 between 1901 and 1907, along with about 38,000 who remigrated from Hawaii to the mainland. Women constituted only 4 percent of the mainland Japanese in 1900, but rose to 13 percent in 1910, and 35 percent in 1920. Most of that increase was due to the migration of picture brides, who escaped the restrictions of the Gentlemen's Agreement.

Many of the Japanese who arrived in Hawaii and the U.S. mainland after 1908 were the children and wives of men admitted before exclusion. "I was six years old when my father went to the United States," recalled Tokushiga Kizuka. "Eleven years later . . . my father summoned me to work. My father came to meet me when I landed in San Francisco. Other than a picture, I had no idea how my father looked, and I did not recognize him—it was like we were strangers." Another group of strangers were wives and husbands, most of whom met for the first time at the docks in Honolulu, Seattle, and San Francisco. Remembering her journey to America, Rikae Inouye observed that "most of the people on board were picture brides. I came with my husband. When the boat anchored, one girl took out a picture from her kimono sleeve and said to me, 'Mrs. Inouye, will you let me know if you see this face?' She was darling. Putting the picture back into her kimono sleeve, she went out to the deck. The men who had come to pick up their brides were there. It was like that. I felt they were bold." But picture brides were sometimes tricked into unhappy marriages. "The picture brides were full of ambition, expectation, and dreams," recalled Ai Miyasaki. "None knew what their husbands were like except by the photos. I wondered how many would be saddened and disillusioned," she speculated. "There were many. The grooms were not what the women thought they were. The men would say that they had businesses and send pictures which were taken when they were younger and deceived the brides. In reality, the men carried blanket rolls on their backs and were farm laborers. The men lied about their age and wrote they were fifteen years younger than they actually were."[12]

One of those who carried a blanket roll was Sadame Inouye, who was typical of the thousands of migrant Japanese agricultural workers in the American West. Inouye landed in California after a two-day transit stop in Hawaii. After only a night in San Francisco, he boarded a boat for a Japanese work camp on an island near Stockton on the Sacramento River. "First we worked in the onion fields for a month or so," Inouye recalled. "Then we went to a neighboring island to dig potatoes. It was about August when we finished the job and came up to Sacramento to work until the middle of September, when we went to pick grapes." Agricultural labor ceased during the winter, but in early spring, Inouye picked peas and planted tomatoes in San Leandro. In June and July, he and several others cleared fields of trees and stumps for fifty cents per tree. "When I worked here and there," he explained, "I carried my own blanket roll with me and slept where I could. Sometimes I stayed in boarding houses." In the fall, Inouye headed south to work in a railroad section gang near Santa Barbara, and later cut celery in Santa Ana. After celery season, he picked strawberries in Gardena, and eventually worked for a Japanese farmer in Venice for about six months.[13]

Masuo Akizuki joined his father in California in 1912. "When I came

to San Jose the day after my arrival," he noted, "everybody was working in the countryside. The boarding houses in San Jose Japantown
found jobs for us. They brought us by horse carriage to the place to
work, and we each were given one blanket. Our living conditions were
miserable at that time. We slept next to a horse stable on our blan-
kets and some straw. . . . When we finished the work, we went back
to the boarding house and rested there until the next job came
around."[14] "The camps are worse than dog and pig pens," wrote a Japanese reporter after visiting agricultural work camps near Fresno. "They
are totally unfit for human beings to sleep in. . . . No one, not even
dirt-poor peasants, wants to live in such unpleasant and filthy sur-
roundings. These camps are the reason why so many robust workers
become ill and die."[15]

Women joined men in that life of labor. Kane Kozono joined her
husband in Alameda, where he worked as a gardener and she as a
domestic servant: "I was paid five dollars a week for the housework
I was doing there. . . . I was settling into the life there fairly well, but
we moved to Sacramento, where some of my husband's relatives were
working on a farm. My husband started growing onions, and together
with a friend of ours, I worked there digging onions, putting them
in a sack, and so forth. I was young then and could do the hard work."
But Kozono did both field and household labor, unlike her husband,
and bearing and rearing children required constant attention. "After
I had babies, raising children was another big job," she affirmed.
"Whenever I went to work, I took them with me to the ranch, and
I would leave them sleeping under a tree. . . . And when the day's
work was over, I would carry one of them on my back to our home.
Men had to work only while they were out in the field," she said point-
edly, "whereas I had to do all those things besides my share of work
in the field. I did their laundry after work too. It was a really gruel-
ing, hard time for me."[16]

On a typical workday on their tomato farm, Kimiko Ono and her
husband woke up before sunrise and picked the day's harvest until
about 6:30 A.M., when she stopped to prepare breakfast for the family. After breakfast, her husband left to sell the tomatoes, and she, with
her three children, watered and tended the tomato plants in the green-
house. "Even when the children were tired of playing and fussed, I
couldn't quit and go to them," Ono recalled sadly. "Meanwhile, the

crying voices would stop, and many times I found my youngsters sleeping on the ground. Telling myself, 'Poor little things! When you grow up I will let you do whatever you want to do . . . only please forgive your mama now. . . .' I worked continually." Ono's husband returned from market about 7 P.M., and after dinner, she put the children to bed. She then sorted tomatoes and packed them in boxes. Turning in at midnight was an early bedtime. A farmer and mother, Ono was also a poet. She wrote,

> Both my hands grimy,
> Unable to wipe away
> The sweat from my brow,
> Using one arm as towel—
> That was I . . . working . . . working.[17]

As Japanese Americans sank their roots into America's soil, working, working, others strove to uproot them. "Once in Riverside I went into a barbershop, sat there, and started to read a newspaper," remembered Kengo Tajima. "While I was reading, the barber came and said, 'We don't serve you.' When I found out I wasn't wanted, I went out. I didn't know that Japanese were not wanted." Heitaro Hikida recalled: "Not a single Japanese was allowed to enter the Alki Beach or the shore at Ballard" in Washington State. "Also, we were discriminated against in the high class movie houses and theaters. They would never refuse us entry outright, but would simply never sell us a first class seat. Instead they gave us balcony seats." "I went to a theater on Third Avenue with my wife and friends," Sentaro Tsuboi added. "We were all led up to the second balcony with the Blacks." Reflecting on his early years in America, Choichi Nitta exclaimed: "There was so much anti-Japanese feeling in those days! They called us 'Japs' and threw things at us. When I made a trip to Marysville to look for land, someone threw rocks. It took strong determination to decide to buy land and live here permanently."[18]

Determination alone, however, was insufficient at times. States passed alien land laws that denied property rights to "aliens ineligible to citizenship," a euphemism that applied to Asians only because the U.S. Constitution, the Supreme Court held in 1922, limited naturalization to Whites and Blacks. California's 1913 alien land law denied

Asians the right to buy property in the state, and its 1920 version prohibited them the ability to rent land. Like African Americans and Latinos, Asians faced a range of discriminatory laws and social practices that included segregated housing and schools, limited opportunities in education and employment, denial of free access to certain public facilities, and bearing the stigma of a supposed racial inferiority. "I am a fruitstand worker," a nisei wrote in 1937. "It is not a very attractive nor distinguished occupation. . . . I would much rather it were doctor or lawyer . . . but my aspiration of developing into such [was] frustrated long ago. . . . I am only what I am, a professional carrot washer."[19]

The most basic right from which stemmed much of the institutionalized discrimination was the denial of U.S. citizenship to the first-generation Japanese. But even the second generation, the nisei, who were American citizens by birth, felt the sting of racism that led to feelings of marginality and self-hatred. A large number of his generation, a twenty-three-year-old nisei confided in 1939, "are, or try to be, intensely 'American.' They have adopted American conventions with a vengeance . . . some are ashamed of their parents' culture, and sometimes even of them as persons. . . . But their faces remain Japanese; and I have been told that some in this 'Americanized' element suffer occasionally before the mirrors in the privacy of their room, for their standards of facial and bodily characteristics also are 'American' or Caucasian." Despite the second generation's attempts to maintain a proper sense of dignity and self-worth, the nisei essayist observed, racism kept them off-balance with its grating intrusions of inferiority. "You know how the cable cars groan and grind and jangle and rattle," he wrote. "All those discordant noises cut through any objectiveness I ever experienced." And he mused, "I rode uphill in a cable car. . . . I thought of my brother, of the artistic arrangement of fruits and vegetables in that store where he worked, of the fruits of the earth brought together and arranged in a pattern of beauty, harmony and color. . . . The car groaned and jangled."[20]

The acculturation of the nisei, their "Americanization," took place primarily in the public schools that were open to Japanese Americans since 1907, when President Theodore Roosevelt pressured the San Francisco school board to rescind its segregation of Japanese students into Oriental schools and thereby averted an international conflict with Japan. By the early 1930s, according to a Stanford University survey of niseis over twenty years of age, the average length of schooling for men was 12.5 years and for women, 12.0; and it found that the nisei held high vocational aspirations. Many saw education as a means to escape grinding farm work, and aspired to become doctors, dentists, pharmacists, and engineers, or sought entry into business and the skilled trades.[21] Those nisei ambitions were tempered, nonetheless, by the recognition that certain fields were closed to them.

Closures sometimes inspired massive resistance on the part of those excluded, as when 8,300 Filipino and Japanese sugar plantation workers on Oahu struck for higher wages and equality in the workplace. That 1920 strike affirmed for some in government the domestic menace posed by the Japanese that was couched in the popular and ill-defined phrase, the "yellow peril." Hawaii's planters described the strike as "an attempt on the part of the Japanese to obtain control of the sugar industry" and as "a dark conspiracy to Japanize this American territory," and a federal commission sent by Washington reported that the strike warned of "the spectre of alien domination." "One of the most important features about this strike . . . ," wrote the head of military intelligence in Hawaii, "was the methods used by the Japanese in carrying on the strike. These methods brought home to the Americans the fact that when the Japanese have decided upon a course of action they allow nothing in the world to stop them from gaining their objective."[22] Had the strikers seen those secret documents, they would have been amazed. The strike involved Filipinos as well as Japanese, and the workers' demands included higher wages for men and women, an eight-hour day, an eight-week paid maternity leave for women, and improved health-care and recreational facilities.

A few months before the 1920 strike, a report by an agent of the Bureau of Investigation, the forerunner of the Federal Bureau of Investigation, contended that Japan had embarked upon a "program for world supremacy" and used California as a dumping ground for its "constantly increasing surplus population." If the tide of immigration was not halted, warned the report, "the white race, in no long space of time, would be driven from the state, and California eventually become a province of Japan." Further, "it would be only a question of time until the entire Pacific coast region would be controlled by the Japanese." Not content with America's West Coast,

Japan planned a global race war. "It is the determined purpose of Japan," the report alleged, "to amalgamate the entire colored races of the world against the Nordic or white race, with Japan at the head of the coalition, for the purpose of wrestling away the supremacy of the white race and placing such supremacy in the colored peoples under the dominion of Japan."[23]

Those notions moved beyond mere rhetoric, albeit secret and highly classified, when during the 1920s the Bureau and military drew up plans for the identification, removal, and detention of key figures among Hawaii's Japanese. In 1922, the Bureau listed, under the heading "Japanese Espionage—Hawaii," 157 Japanese, including merchants, Buddhist priests, Japanese-language school principals and teachers, laborers, Christian ministers, and others. A year later, Hawaii's military planned the defense of the islands in a war with Japan that involved a declaration of martial law, the registration of all enemy aliens, the internment of those considered to be security risks, information censorship, and controls over movement and labor. By the decade's end, the military considered all Japanese, both aliens and citizens alike, as enemy aliens, and its criterion for internment changed from espionage to leadership. There was no need to determine whether a person was guilty of espionage or even had the potential for espionage; the military held that guilt, thus internment, was simply determined by that person's position of leadership in the community. Stripped of its leaders, the military planners reasoned, Hawaii's Japanese would be easily controlled.[24]

President Franklin D. Roosevelt joined in those preparations when in 1936 he wrote to the military's Joint Board chief in Washington: "Has the local Joint Planning Committee (Hawaii) any recommendation to make? One obvious thought occurs to me—that every Japanese citizen or non-citizen on the Island of Oahu who meets these Japanese ships or has any connection with their officers or men should be secretly but definitely identified and his or her name placed on a special list of those who would be the first to be placed in a concentration camp in the event of trouble." The occasion for the president's "obvious thought" was an intelligence report from Hawaii about visits by Japanese naval ships in Hawaiian ports and the entertainment of those sailors by the local Japanese. After having read the report, the president asked to be informed about "what arrangements and plans have been made relative to concentration camps in the Hawaiian Islands for dangerous or undesirable aliens or citizens in the event of [a] national emergency." The acting secretary of war responded to the president's concern by informing him that Hawaii's military had created a unified "Service Command" of military and civilian forces for "the control of the civil population and the prevention of sabotage, of civil disturbances, or of local uprisings" by "potentially hostile Japanese." And the Joint Board assured the president: "It is a routine matter for those responsible for military intelligence to maintain lists of suspects, who will normally be the first to be interned under the operation of the Joint Defense Plan, Hawaiian Theater, in the event of war." But the Board also stressed the need for constant vigilance, and recommended greater coordination among the various departments of government. Roosevelt thus formed a committee consisting of the attorney general and the secretaries of war, state, treasury, labor, and navy "to work out some practical solution to the problem" of interagency cooperation in curbing the alleged Japanese danger.[25]

Like their counterparts in Hawaii, military and civilian intelligence on the mainland had surveyed "the Japanese problem" at least since World War I. That surveillance of West Coast Japanese Americans rose in urgency after the 1920 sugar strike in Hawaii and again after Japan's invasion of Manchuria in 1931. By mid-1941, the Justice Department had a list of over 2,000 mainland Japanese who were marked for detention because, like those in Hawaii, they were among the leaders of their communities. They also included those whose jobs were considered to be vital to the national security, such as fishermen who owned boats with shortwave radios and who knew the coastal waters, but also farmers and produce distributors.[26]

Neither Roy Nakata nor Alice Sinclair Dodge could have known about those plans by the leaders of their government, but their lives would soon bear the impress of their implementation. The nation's leaders were rightly concerned about Japan's imperialism in Asia, but they wrongly conceived of that aggression in racial terms—as a war launched by peoples of color, led by Japan, against white supremacy—and hence consigned Japanese Americans, as an undifferentiated "racial" group, to the opposing side of the binary racial divide. The formulation equated the Japanese in America with Japan, and peoples of color with antiwhite; and because, in that equation, America was synonymous with Whites, Japanese Americans were anti-American.

Those equivalences, however, had to be made, spread, and repeated before they could reach the level of truth, indeed of an assumption, within the popular imagination. As Mary Tsukamoto astutely observed, having witnessed the anti-Japanese movement of the 1920s and 1930s, "Prejudice was deliberately manufactured, and people had to work hard to create and stir it up." Patriotic organizations, like the Native Sons and Daughters of the Golden West and American Legion, she remembered, along with the California Federation of Labor and the Hearst and McClatchy newspapers, "all claimed that the Japanese were going to own all of California, that we were going to take over the land."[27] Popular novels by Sax Rohmer introduced the evil genius Fu Manchu, "the yellow peril incarnate," whose aim was to subdue "the white world," and intellectuals like Lothrop Stoddard warned of a "rising tide of color" that threatened white supremacy and thus constituted "the crisis of the ages."[28] Surely, the resemblances between the secret thoughts and plans of the government and the "yellow peril" and white supremacist discourses that were aimed at the public must have been more than coincidental. And, as pointed out by Mary Tsukamoto, America's Japanese "were innocent victims, but we have to understand this background if we are to understand what happened when the war broke out."[29]

Japan's attack on Pearl Harbor surprised many Japanese Americans. "I got up at 9:00 that morning," remembered a nisei of December 7, 1941. "Everyone in the household was out in the yard shouting and pointing towards the sky. I hurried downstairs to see what was the matter and my mother was the first to tell me that the 'Japs' had come. My reaction was one of complete disbelief. Even after I had looked towards the sky and had seen planes flying overhead and had heard the sound of cannon fire, I was still convinced that the army and navy were on maneuvers. I was so firm in my arguments that half of the family were ready to believe me until the radio announcer uttered the fatal words that we were being attacked by the 'Japs.' My mother kept running up and down the house, muttering a prayer as she did."[30]

On the mainland, Kiyo Hirano and her children went to bed looking forward to Sunday. "That morning, as usual, I woke up at six and prepared breakfast," she recalled. "Around ten, a phone call came from a friend who told me in a hysterical voice, *'Taihen, taihen;* a terrible thing has happened! The Japanese planes are bombing Pearl Harbor! Hurry up and listen to the radio!' Still not believing, I turned on the radio. . . . That whole day I spent speechless, seated in front of the radio. I will never forget that morning of December 7th, 1941." Hirano also remembered that her white neighbors were similarly shocked by Japan's attack. Some Whites "who had been our friends just a day before," she noted, "were those who now turned into enemies," but there were other Whites who told Hirano, "'We have nothing against you. What wrong have you committed?'"[31]

The *San Francisco Chronicle,* a paper notable for its anti-Japanese rhetoric, having warned its readers of a "Japanese invasion" in February 1905, editorialized on December 9, 1941: "The roundup of Japanese citizens in various parts of the country . . . is not a call for volunteer spy hunters to go into action. Neither is it a reason to lift an eyebrow at a Japanese, whether American-born or not. . . . There is no excuse to wound the sensibilities of any persons in America by showing suspicion or prejudice. That, if anything, is a help to fifth column spirit. An American-born Nazi would like nothing better than to set the dogs of prejudice on a first-class American Japanese."[32]

And church groups cautioned against scapegoating. Two days after Pearl Harbor, the presidents of the Federal Council of the Churches of Christ in America, the Foreign Missions Conference of North America, and the Home Missions Council of North America issued a joint public statement. "Under the emotional strain of the moment," they warned, "Americans will be tempted to express their resentment against the action of Japan's government by recriminations against the Japanese people who are in our midst. . . . Let us remember that many of these people are loyal, patriotic American citizens and that others, though Japanese subjects, have been utterly opposed to their nation's acts against our nation. It is incumbent upon us to demonstrate a discipline which, while carefully observing the precautions necessary to national safety, has no place for vindictiveness."[33]

Kiyo Hirano was the domestic servant of a white military family. The husband was a first lieutenant stationed at San Francisco's Presidio when the war broke out, and his wife was in her late teens with an infant daughter. "The missus depended on me and turned to me for everything," Hirano noted. "I, an enemy alien. My employers, American and in the military." After Pearl Harbor, the lieutenant was sent to the Pacific theater, where his ship was sunk by a Japanese torpedo. "It was a week later when I saw the missus again," Hirano remembered. "When she saw me, she grabbed me, crying, 'I no longer have a husband.' . . . My heart felt a sharp pain as though pierced by a thick steel rod. Speechless, we just embraced each other and cried. A few days later, the missus and her baby returned to her parents' home in San Diego. On the day of her departure, the missus told me, 'Though my stay in Sausalito has been short, whenever I think of this place, I will think of you. The day of peace cannot be so far away. We may meet again. Take care.'"[34]

The "dogs of prejudice" weren't unleashed by Hirano's employers but by those in government, some of whom held scant regard for the precious rights of citizenship. As Assistant Secretary of War John J. McCloy put it during a meeting of representatives from the Justice and War Departments, "If it is a question of the safety of the country [and] the Constitution. . . . Why the Constitution is just a scrap of paper to me."[35] McCloy's outburst was in response to the Justice Department's insistence that it did not approve of the mass removal of Japanese American citizens and instead favored action against enemy aliens only. Still, Attorney General Francis Biddle's attempts to forestall the Army's determination to evict all Japanese Americans from the West Coast was not prompted by constitutional concerns over the rights of citizens but by pragmatic ones over whether such a program was necessary and how it could be handled. Biddle was adamant in his refusal to involve the Justice Department in the deed of Japanese American removal, but he did not block the Army's assumption of authority in that matter.[36]

The plans, formulated over two decades, were put into operation. "Immediately take into custody all Japanese who have been classified in A, B, and C categories in material previously transmitted to you," the FBI teletype instructed on the evening of December 7. "Take immediate action and advise Bureau frequently as to exact identity of persons arrested. Persons taken into custody should be turned over to the nearest representative of the Immigration and Naturalization Service." By December 9, 1,291 Japanese, 865 Germans, and 147 Italians were in custody in Hawaii and on the U.S. mainland.

"My husband, Setsuzo, and I were picked up by the FBI early in the morning of December 8, 1941, in Idaho Falls because we were Japanese-language teachers and my husband was the secretary of the Japanese Association, an organization assisting Issei needing help in interpreting business and legal problems," Take Uchida recalled. "We were taken to the Seattle Immigration office immediately. We were not given a chance to store our belongings or furniture—just enough time to finish breakfast." Her husband was sent from Seattle to an internment camp in Bismarck, North Dakota, and Uchida remained in Seattle until April 1942, when she was transferred to the Federal Women's Penitentiary in Seagoville, Texas, where she joined other Japanese internees, women and children from Peru and Panama, and where she later met women detainees sent from Hawaii. "Most of the ladies were schoolteachers and the educated wives of influential businessmen engaged in business with Japan," Uchida explained.[37]

Those detentions of community leaders, along with occasional raids for contraband, including cameras, binoculars, knives, and guns, created fear among Japanese Americans and encouraged paranoia among their white neighbors. In Seattle, Christian minister Daisuke Kitagawa recalled visiting the families of those who had been interned. "In no time," he testified, "the whole community was thoroughly panic-stricken; every male lived in anticipation of arrest by the FBI, and every household endured each day in fear and trembling. Most Japanese, including at least one clergyman, were so afraid of being marked by association with those who had been taken away that they hesitated to visit the wives and children of the victims. Much of that fear can be attributed to the rumors, rampant in the community," explained Kitagawa, "about the grounds for those arrests, about the treatment the detainees were getting, and about their probable imprisonment for the duration of the war. No rational explanation could set their minds at ease."[38]

Instead, Whites stepped into the breach to help their fellow Americans. "In a few cases," wrote Everett W. Thompson, a Christian minister in Seattle, "we were present when an arrest was made and were able to help as interpreters. In many more, we called at the home shortly afterward to reassure the family that such an arrest was not a disgrace and that we had all confidence in the integrity of the arrested man. Next, calls were made on the men themselves in the local jail, and even several hundred miles away at the camps where they were being kept. . . . Many pastors and church workers had a share in arranging bank accounts or guaranteeing people now under suspicion because the FBI had taken their husbands or fathers, or merely translating and interpreting in business arrangements."[39]

In the nation's capital, the process of assigning blame for the Pearl Harbor disaster was under way. Despite the conclusion of the Army's board of inquiry that there was "no single instance of sabotage" and "in no case was there any instance of misbehavior" on the part of Hawaii's Japanese, Secretary of the Navy Frank Knox told the press in mid-December that Pearl Harbor resulted from "the most effective fifth column work that's come out of this war, except in Norway." In January, Knox asked the secretary of war to provide "information as to [the] practicability of concentration of local Japanese nationals . . . on some island other than Oahu," and the following month, during a cabinet meeting, he proposed the internment of all of Oahu's Japanese on the island of Molokai.[40]

But martial law had been declared in Hawaii hours after Japan's attack, as had been planned since the 1920s, and those less inclined than Knox to salvage the Navy's honor by displacing blame onto Oahu's Japanese pointed out that without their labor the islands' economy would falter and possibly collapse. No, they argued successfully, the detention of Hawaii's Japanese leaders and the controls imposed under martial law were sufficient for their containment and assurance of their utility as workers. Japanese on the mainland's West Coast, by contrast, comprised a small percentage of the population and were not as vital economically as those in Hawaii. Indeed, there was some sentiment for their removal among politicians, patriotic groups, and agricultural interests. "We're charged with wanting to get rid of the Japs for selfish reasons," Austin Anson, the managing secretary of California's Grower-Shipper Vegetable Association, was quoted as saying in May 1942. "We might as well be honest. We do. It's a question of whether the white man lives on the Pacific Coast or the brown men. . . . If all the Japs were removed tomorrow, we'd never miss them in two weeks, because the white farmers can take over and produce everything the Jap grows. And we don't want them back when the war ends, either."[41]

President Roosevelt, who like Navy Secretary Knox and Secretary of War Henry L. Stimson had worried for years over the dangers posed by Hawaii's Japanese, decided to allow the military to determine the fate of the Japanese living along the West Coast. Stimson's assistant, John J. McCloy, reported to the Army's Western Defense Command in San Francisco that the war secretary had spoken with the president on the afternoon of February 11, 1942, and Roosevelt had instructed him to "go ahead and do anything you think necessary . . . if it involves citizens, we will take care of them too. He [the president] says there will probably be some repercussions, but it has got to be dictated by military necessity, but as he puts it, 'Be as reasonable as you can.'"[42] As McCloy had promised, on February 19, 1942, Roosevelt indeed signed Executive Order 9066, which authorized the military to designate areas from which "any or all persons may be excluded" and to provide for such persons "transportation, food, shelter, and other accommodations as may be necessary . . . to accomplish the purpose of this order." Thus it was that with high school graduation in sight, Roy Nakata contemplated the prospect of "being sent to an internment camp and wasting away what little knowledge I have gained thus far, as well as the much precious time."

Five days before Executive Order 9066, the Navy ordered about 500 families of Japanese on Terminal Island, in the port of Los Angeles, to vacate their homes within a month. The islanders, mainly fishermen and cannery workers, were prime targets for exclusion because of the location of their homes adjacent to the Long Beach Naval Station and because the fishermen knew the coastal waters and had boats with shortwave radios. Many of the men were among those apprehended by the FBI shortly after Pearl Harbor, and as they were being taken away, Virginia Swanson, a Baptist missionary on the island, reported that "the families huddled together sorrowing and weeping."[43] On February 25, without warning, new notices were posted informing the islanders that they had until midnight February 27 to vacate their homes. "Near-panic swept the community," wrote Bill Hosokawa, "particularly those where the family head was in custody. Word spread quickly and human vultures in the guise of used-furniture dealers descended on the island. They drove up and down the streets in trucks offering $5 for a nearly new washing machine, $10 for refrigerators."[44] A nisei volunteer who helped the islanders pack recalled: "The women cried awful. . . . Some of them smashed their stuff, broke it up, right before the buyers' eyes because they offered such ridiculous prices."[45]

Virginia Swanson phoned the Navy to get the deadline extended. The Navy refused. She appealed to members of Congress, Justice Department heads, Eleanor Roosevelt, and the West Coast military to ensure that the evicted Terminal Islanders would find homes in communities receptive to them, and asked, "Could you work to find a place where they could move? Can you be sure families won't be broken up?"[46] She received no reply. Because the government failed to be accountable for the results of its order, Swanson and others, including nisei volunteers, Ralph Mayberry of the Baptist Mission Board, Esther Rhoads and Herbert Nicholson of the American Friends Service Committee, and Allan Hunter, a Congregational minister, secured moving trucks and located and prepared Japanese-language school halls and other temporary shelters for the islanders.

"The volunteers with trucks worked all night," Swanson reported. "The people had to go, ready or not. Some had to be pulled forcibly from their homes. They were afraid they were going to be handed over to a firing squad. Why should they have believed me," she asked, "telling them to get into trucks with strangers?" At the Forsyth School, one of the reception centers readied by the volunteers for the exiled people, Esther Rhoads was among the workers and described the scene. "All afternoon trucks and Japanese kept coming. They were tired and dazed as a result of the sudden exodus. . . . We have old men over seventy—retired fishermen whom the FBI considered ineffective, and we have little children—one baby a year old . . . practically no men between thirty-five and sixty-five, as they all are interned. . . . Where are these people to go?" she asked. "There are many Japanese with young leaders able to face pioneer life, but those who have come to our hostels represent a group too old or too young to stand the rigors of beginning all over again."[47] And Terminal Island was just a dress rehearsal for the massive eviction program that would affect so many lives.

Toward a Better Society

"EVACUATION! What does *that* mean to the American people? I'm sure it doesn't mean as much as it did to me," wrote Tomiko Sato. "Evacuation meant leaving my home and friends and boarding a bus to reside at North Portland Assembly Center on May 20, 1942. How well I remember that day. As I trudged with others into the fenced and guarded center and heard the gate clang shut behind me, a lump came to my throat, but I noticed some friends waving to me, so new courage sprang up within me."

About three months later, Sato and her family moved from the assembly center to Minidoka Relocation Center in southern Idaho, one of the ten concentration camps administered by the civilian War Relocation Authority (WRA). "It was built like a regular army camp—barracks, mess halls and laundries," recalled Sato of Minidoka. "But the main dislikes of everyone were the terrific dust during the dry season and the sloppy mud during the rainy seasons."

"I applied for an indefinite release to attend North Idaho Junior College in Coeur d'Alene," Sato continued her story, "and after waiting three long tedious months permission finally came through. February 2 I left Minidoka and reached here in time to attend the last semester of school. I was introduced to everyone at school and from then on I knew I would love Coeur d'Alene as well as I did my home town of Beaverton, Oregon. The faculty and students were the nicest and friendliest I've ever associated with."

Sato ended her statement, published in February 1944, with: "My future is very rosy, for with all my American friends about me I feel as if I'm one of them. It is with *great* emphasis that I say—'Hats Off!' to America and her sailors, soldiers, and marines. I'm glad I am an American."[1]

After the Terminal Island evictions, the Army moved methodically from north to south starting with another group of islanders, the several hundred Japanese on Bainbridge Island near Seattle, who were forcibly removed from their homes in March 1942. Soldiers in battle fatigues tacked up posters, "Instructions to All Persons of Japanese Ancestry," on the island's utility poles, at the post office, and at the ferry landing. Mostly berry and truck farmers, the Bainbridge Japanese were given six days to close their farms and pack their possessions. Lieutenant General John L. DeWitt, head of the Western Defense Command, had issued proclamations that divided Washington, Oregon, California, and Arizona into military areas from which, under Executive Order 9066, enemy aliens and all Japanese—aliens and citizens—were to be excluded, and instituted an 8 P.M. to 6 A.M. curfew for the targeted peoples.

It was a "raw, overcast day," wrote Bill Hosokawa of March 30, 1942. "Although the Japanese had been given less than a week in which to settle their affairs and pack," he reported of the Bainbridge Islanders, "they began to gather at the assembly point long before the designated hour, each of the fifty-four families carrying only the meager items authorized by the Army—bedding, linens, toilet articles, extra clothing, enamel plates and eating utensils. All else, the possessions collected over a lifetime, had to be stored with friends, delivered to a government warehouse, sold or abandoned. Farms developed over decades were leased or simply left to be overgrown by weeds."[2] Armed soldiers directed the people to the waiting ferryboat that would take them to Seattle. As the ferry pulled away from the dock, there must have been many tear-filled eyes riveted on their island home as it receded in the shrouded distance.

"Several weeks before May," remembered Mrs. Takae Washizu in Sacramento, California, "soldiers came around and posted notices on telephone poles. It was sad for me to leave the place where I had been living for such a long time. Staring at the ceiling in bed at night, I wondered who would take care of my cherry tree and my house after we moved out. I also thought about my mother in Japan." The soldiers, Washizu recalled, "were mean" and "whenever I did something wrong, they put the muzzle of their rifle on my long hair." On the day of their departure, Washizu and her fellow Sacramento Japanese were given sandwiches, oranges, and milk for lunch, and, she noted, "each family was given a number."[3]

The Bainbridge Islanders and Sacramento Japanese, like Roy Nakata and Tomiko Sato's families, were first taken to places called assembly centers managed by the Army's Wartime Civil Control Administration (WCCA). These were temporary holding shelters, generally at county fairgrounds and horse racetracks, in places like Puyallup (Washington); Portland (Oregon); Marysville, Sacramento, Stockton, Tanforan, Turlock, Merced, Pinedale, Salinas, Fresno, Tulare, Santa Anita, and Pomona (California); and Camp Mayer (Arizona). The deed was completed by August 1942. From those assembly centers, the Japanese were transported to the WRA-run concentration camps scattered in the American interior: Tule Lake and Manzanar (California), Minidoka (Idaho), Topaz (Utah), Poston and Gila River (Arizona), Heart Mountain (Wyoming), Amache (Colorado), and Rohwer and Jerome (Arkansas).

In March 1942, about a month after Executive Order 9066 was issued, a group of educators expressed concern over the impending removal of Japanese from the West Coast, including their nisei college and university students. At institutions with substantial numbers of nisei students, presidents such as Lee Paul Sieg of the University of Washington, Robert Gordon Sproul of the University of California, Berkeley, and Remsen Bird of Occidental College met with faculty, students, and church people to discuss ways that would allow the approximately 2,500 nisei students affected by the exclusion orders to complete their education.

The first conference to discuss nisei student relocation was held March 21, 1942, at the YMCA of the University of California, Berkeley. Members agreed that their greatest immediate need was a coordinated effort among the diverse individuals and groups working on student relocation. They resolved to establish a central office for the Student Relocation Committee with funds applied for from the YMCA and YWCA, and recommended the hiring of Joseph Conard, a Berkeley graduate student at the time, to act as its executive secretary. Located at Berkeley, the central office would serve as a clearinghouse for the three area groups working independently in the Pacific Northwest, northern California, and southern California. Finally, the group urged the government to exempt students from the wholesale removal, and when that appeal failed, members worked to have students transfer to campuses east of the exclusion zone.

In arguing the case for the group, Sproul stressed the importance of the nisei students as future leaders of the Japanese American community, and noted that government sponsorship of their education, including scholarships, was an "insurance on the future welfare of the American Nation."[4] That contention would ultimately prove persuasive with influential government officials and foundation and church heads who enabled and underwrote much of the student relocation effort.

Those West Coast educators concerned with nisei education were joined by some of their colleagues in the Midwest. On March 18, 1942, W. C. Coffey, president of the University of Minnesota, wrote to seventeen of his fellow presidents in the Midwest as well as some as far east as Cornell University in Ithaca, New York. The main body of Coffey's letter was directed at the hiring of "refugee Germans," but he also asked for advice on "our willingness to accept as graduate students, Americans of Japanese extraction who may be forced to leave the restricted areas on the west coast. Have you considered this matter at all?" he asked. Coffey hoped that "there were some way we could reach a policy in these matters to which we could all agree."[5]

The University of Illinois's Arthur C. Willard reported that he suspected that his institution's board of trustees would not "look with favor upon the admission of either Japanese aliens or Americans of Japanese ancestry. We have had some problems of our own along this line and naturally are reluctant to take on any more such responsibilities," he explained. "It is unfortunate, of course, that American citizens of the Japanese race must suffer because of the aggression of the country of their ancestors," Willard continued, "but on the other hand, it would be a mistake to place them in a position wherein the public would feel, rightly or wrongly, that they were being given special privileges and protection."[6]

In contrast, Deane W. Malott, chancellor of the University of Kansas, responded that he was "entirely willing" to admit Japanese American students. "I think possibly my own attitude is caused somewhat by the fact that I lived in Hawaii for a number of years and know many fine Americans there of Japanese extraction," Malott reflected. However, the matter rested with the board of regents and was currently under consideration. "Kansas is a rather conservative state," the chancellor observed, "and I think the Regents are somewhat concerned as to the attitude of the people." The regents, he concluded, would likely follow "the attitude" of the FBI, with whom they had consulted. But, Malott urged, the nisei were American citizens and "we must take care of them."[7]

The regents of the University of Colorado, Boulder, considered the appeals of several West Coast university and college presidents on behalf of their nisei students. During its meeting of March 20, 1942, the regents shaped a policy that allowed "a number" of Japanese American students to be admitted provided they were U.S. citizens and self-supporting, paid nonresident tuition, were cleared by the FBI and Navy, were in good standing at their originating institutions, and were prohibited from attending classes "the subject matter of which is of a confidential nature." During its July 10, 1942, meeting, the regents heard the president's assistant present a more detailed plan of admissions. The University of Colorado, the plan determined, would admit a maximum of sixty out-of-state nisei students, and they would be distributed as follows: not more than two students in medicine, three in law, twelve in engineering, five in business, five in pharmacy, eight in nursing, four in music, eighteen in arts and sciences, and three in the graduate school.[8] In that way, the president hoped, clusters of Japanese American students wouldn't draw attention to themselves and thereby subject the institution to public criticism.

Grinnell College in Iowa was an early supporter of nisei student relocation. In a letter dated May 2, 1942, from Joseph Conard to his uncle Henry Conard, the West Coast executive secretary reported that the relocation committee had received "many good offers from the Middle West, but none equaling Grinnell's with board, room and tuition for two students." Conard's letter also outlined the procedure during this phase of student relocation, when Japanese Americans were still living in prohibited and restricted zones controlled by the military before being moved to detention camps. Students had to be accepted by institutions outside the military zone, demonstrate their ability to pay the costs of their education, and secure the Army's approval for travel. When approval was granted, students were not "released" from the military's control, but were considered by the Army to remain under its "protective custody."

Conard was concerned about nisei students as individuals. Some of the students, especially one who had been accepted by Grinnell, "have heard frightening rumors of racial prejudice in the Midwest, and will perhaps show undue nervousness because of the great uncertainties they face. Many will be worried about their families, and many, if not all, will be coming for the first time far from home without any clear knowledge as to when they can rejoin their people." The father of that particular student, Conard reported, had been arrested by the FBI and was being held in detention, and despite the fact that his father's situation had scant bearing on his patriotism or loyalty, the student might be sensitive to what others thought of him or his father. Conard expressed his hope that the student would find a counselor with whom he could have intimate conversations if he chose, and ventured that "it will mean a great deal to be met at the train on arrival."[9]

A week later, Henry Conard reported to his nephew: "The three students arrived duly Friday morning at 4 A.M. Four of the boys from Gates Hall, our housemate, Roberta Lincoln, the hostess from Mears, and I met them at the station." The Gates students invited the nisei young man to live in their hall, and one of the nisei women stayed with the Conards and the other was given lodging in Mears. "The reception of the students has been most cordial," the elder Conard wrote. "I could even say there is great enthusiasm. We all expect to settle down to the routine of life as soon as possible." Life in Grinnell, Iowa, must have been novel to the nisei students, but it must have been equally liberating to leave behind the military restrictions and curfews of California. "I wish thee could see Grinnell at this moment," Conard told his nephew. "The lilacs are in full bloom, the tulips are at their height, and the earliest peonies are gorgeous. . . . It doesn't seem possible that even California can be as splendid as Iowa in May."[10]

The University of Wisconsin's Clarence A. Dykstra suggested to the University of Minnesota's W. C. Coffey that university presidents approach the WRA's director, Milton S. Eisenhower. The relocation of nisei students, he wrote, should be a matter of national policy. If directed by the federal government and if nisei students were distributed widely, most individuals and institutions in the Midwest would find that acceptable, he predicted.[11] Indeed, Coffey presented his concerns in a message to Eisenhower, with copies to the Secretary of War and George F. Zook of the American Council on Education, about the need for a national policy on nisei student relocation. "Urge that Army give immediate attention to problem of Japanese-American students of West Coast areas who are seeking to migrate to inland universities," Coffey cabled Eisenhower. "Numbers have arrived Minnesota University in last three days without any assurance of admittance. Regard it urgent that systematic plan for relocating such individuals be worked out invoking cooperation of large numbers of institutions each willing to accept one or two thus spreading the students." His worry, Coffey explained, involved the fear of a mass migration of students to a single institution, like Minnesota, and the alienation of large numbers of Japanese Americans through the creation of "misunderstandings" in their minds. If a federal agency coordinated that effort, Coffey suggested, educational institutions would be more likely to admit nisei students because the federal mandate would shield them from public criticism.[12]

Those correspondences and discussions initiated by college and university presidents on the West Coast and in the Midwest, and furthered by national bodies like the American Council on Education, the Institute of International Education, and the U.S. Office of Education, recognized the need for "a systematic scheme for the location of Japanese students from the West coast institutions to inland institutions," according to Fred J. Kelly, executive director of the Office of Education Wartime Commission.[13] On April 29, 1942, Zook reported to Coffey that Eisenhower was ready to appoint "an advisory committee" to help the WRA develop a national policy on nisei student relocation. Eisenhower had asked Zook if the American Council on Education had any names to suggest for such a committee. "We believe Mr. Eisenhower to be competent in this job," Zook wrote to Coffey, "and very sympathetic to the plight of the students in whom you are concerned. The Council will help him in every possible way."[14]

On May 5, 1942, Milton Eisenhower contacted Clarence E. Pickett, executive secretary of the American Friends Service Committee in Philadelphia.[15] In his letter, Eisenhower explained the WRA's responsibility for moving Japanese Americans from the prohibited zone, housing them in relocation centers, and educating their children through high school. He noted the advice and efforts of "many eminent educators," who advocated transferring nisei students to institutions away from the exclusion zone. "Certainly I agree that this would be desirable," Eisenhower wrote, but it was "not feasible" for his agency to carry out that project of student relocation. "Consequently," he ventured, "I should like to ask that you establish a committee which would aid you in formulating a set of policies and program."

Eisenhower, of course, knew of the involvement of the American Friends Service Committee on the West Coast with student relocation when he made his request to Pickett. But he also sought a partnership between the WRA, a government agency, and the private sector. "Such a program," Eisenhower explained in his proposal to Pickett, "will involve the selection and certification of students at assembly or relocation centers, a phase of the task that must, of course, be handled by the Federal Government. It will involve transportation of students from the prohibited zone to a designated university, a function which I think may also be handled by [the] WRA. . . . It involves the development of [a] true understanding of this whole problem in many universities making arrangements for the reception of American-citizen Japanese. Finally, it involves either work opportunities or non-Federal funds for the support of students at the universities."[16]

Relocating nisei students presented several complications. The WRA, in charge of the government's effort of mass removal and detention prompted ostensibly by "military necessity," had to reassure certain politicians and the American public that the scattering of Japanese American students throughout the American interior would pose no threat to the national security. Eisenhower thus stressed that "the selection and certification of students" would be undertaken by federal agencies. "Let me emphasize," he wrote in the letter to Pickett, "that the Federal Government [both] for the protection of the students themselves and to re-assure the public will make individual examinations and give individual certifications."[17]

Eisenhower also anticipated that constituencies opposed to nisei student relocation would charge that the government was coddling

Japanese Americans at the very time that white youth were in the bat-
tlefield defending those privileges of education. Thus it was important that the students generate the funds necessary for their education
or that they come from nongovernmental sources. As put by Pickett, Eisenhower believed that financial support of those students by
the government "would bring too much opposition."[18] Indeed, even
Eisenhower's initial, modest pledge of WRA travel support for nisei
students had to be broken in the summer of 1942 because, according to the director of student relocation, "the opposition to any generosity or even decency toward the Japanese is so vociferous in
Washington that to press for an extra point like this will endanger
the entire Japanese welfare program."[19]

The private sector's role, Eisenhower foresaw, was crucial in the
final approval of nisei student relocation by the government. Those
in charge of relocation, he explained to Pickett, had "to see to it that
difficulties would not develop in the new locations to which the students would go."[20] Institutions had to be receptive of Japanese
American students, but also local communities in which those colleges and universities were located. Clearly, institutions had to admit
nisei students, not a given in those days, and student or local community opposition might prove physically dangerous to Japanese
American students and potentially embarrassing to the overall program of relocation. As a student reported to his former mentor at
Duke University in May 1942, "My application was rejected by the
law school faculty. No reason was given but it is obvious. Now that
the government is doing everything possible to help[,] the schools
will not accept us. As I have said before, the government has offered
to pay our train fare. However, this offer will be nullified by the denial
of admittance by the universities."[21]

Despite those strictures that constrained a federal agency, student
relocation was a project that could be embraced by many individuals and groups. As Berkeley's president had argued, the education of
the nisei was an investment in the nation's future. On that, many could
agree. In considering the economic feasibility of Eisenhower's proposal, Pickett listed the potential funding sources for student aid. Many
colleges and universities, he predicted, would provide grants, church
bodies with "a long-standing missionary interest in Japan" would offer
scholarships, several firms "which have done business in Japan and

will want to do business following the war" were another probable source, and private foundations like the Carnegie could be approached. The American Friends Service Committee, Pickett agreed, would carry the main burden of fund-raising.[22]

As if to underscore the wide support for student relocation, Assistant Secretary of War John J. McCloy, an unqualified proponent of the mass removal and detention of the West Coast's Japanese, conveyed to Pickett his endorsement of the project. Eisenhower, he noted, had informed him of the proposal, and "I take great pleasure in advising you that I am in complete sympathy with the suggestions made by Mr. Eisenhower in his letter to you," declared McCloy. "Anything that can legitimately be done to compensate loyal citizens of Japanese ancestry for the dislocation to which they have been subjected, by reason of military necessity, has our full approval. In particular," McCloy continued, "the suggestion for the establishment of a committee of distinguished educators to work out a program of university education in other parts of the country for Japanese-American citizens evacuated from the Pacific Coast meets with my hearty approval."[23]

With those assurances, Pickett invited prominent educators and church people and representatives from the YMCA and YWCA, the American Friends Service Committee, governmental agencies, and the Japanese American Citizens League (a nisei patriotic organization begun in 1930)[24] to meet in Chicago on May 29, 1942. In all, forty-six attended the meeting. The members, according to a digest of the proceedings, were told that there were some 2,300 college and university students in the detention camps, about two-thirds men and one-third women, and that these were "among the best students in the colleges they have left." Because their forced removal and confinement had been "a terrific wrench," it was important that these students be informed of an orderly procedure that might make it possible for them to obtain permits to attend institutions outside restricted areas.

The procedure for student selection revealed some of the principles of the original proposal, that the relocation program, to survive, had to deflect criticism by showing that the nisei were not only exemplary students but also loyal and patriotic American subjects—indeed, a model minority. According to the meeting's digest, each student should be "certified as a loyal citizen" and "selected as a fine student and outstanding representative of the Japanese people." The nisei, in this experiment, were not completely free to act as individuals, because they represented an entire and undifferentiated race or people. They were thus, in the thinking of this group of student relocation planners, goodwill ambassadors. Accordingly, the summary explained the anticipated selection procedures: "academic and personality ratings are equally important in disseminating better attitudes toward the Japanese race. Through interviews, college records and recommendations, careful information should be gathered."[25]

Everyone in charge of student relocation, these planners indicated, must ensure a hospitable environment for the nisei students. This work they called "interpretation." The way must be prepared with the whole community: "Chamber of Commerce, American Legion, Ministerial Board, College Administration, student body, and college faculty." Student placement was an aspect of "interpretation" insofar as student success prompted positive views of the nisei and thereby enhanced their prospects for assimilation. "There should be as careful a choice of colleges as students," the summary report concluded. "If this job is done well, it will spread the understanding of the Japanese and help with their integration into this country."[26]

The Chicago meeting closed by establishing the National Student Relocation Council headed by Robbins W. Barstow, president of Hartford Seminary. It was agreed that the existing West Coast student relocation committees would continue their work, but their efforts would be cleared through the national office on the East Coast. The responsibilities of the Council, agreed upon in Chicago, included selecting students based on both academic qualifications and "personality," locating "cooperating colleges," raising funds for student aid, "preparing [the] atmosphere to receive students," and carefully matching applicants with colleges.[27]

During the summer of 1942, the Council began the work of student selection by drawing up questionnaires to assess student applicants, devising a system of classifying and ranking students on the basis of scholastic merit and personal traits, and securing the official transcripts and records of students. Each applicant was reviewed by two or more staffers and given a composite rating. Those among the highest 15 percent were given priority for admission during the fall 1942 term. Many of those college and university openings were restricted by gender, church membership, class standing, financial status, legal residence, and the availability of courses of study. Students were matched with those opportunities, and in some cases institutions, chosen from a list of qualified applicants.

A volunteer committee of college and university deans and registrars on the West Coast helped to set up the procedures for student selection. Their recommendations appear to have been summarized in a document attributed to Joseph Conard, entitled "Procedure for Analysis of Student Qualifications," as his "suggestions to raters." "We recommend that every student whose application is analyzed be given a 'rating' according to each of two types of promise, 'scholarship' and 'personal factors,' and that in addition to these two figures, there should be a composite rating which combines them," the document noted. Raters should be experienced college admissions personnel, and two of them should review each applicant independently; if their ratings disagreed, a third person should be brought in.[28]

Scholarship was reduced to a grade point average, with no differentiation made based on the "quality" of the schools that granted those grades; and "personal factors" was defined as "the sum-total of all the elements that enter into personality and adaptability and general promise where not related to scholastic ability. This includes the capacity of the student to make a good impression and also his capacity to wear well over a period of time." The document continued: "Maturity, self-reliance, adaptability are important. Reliability, diligence, special interests, leadership, evidence of successful Caucasian contacts and contribution to the Japanese community are all important." Those admittedly "subjective judgments," the document explained, were to be employed to rate applicants as "outstanding" to "below average." The applicant's composite rating was calculated by multiplying the scholastic rating by three and the personal factors rating by two and adding those sums.

Those figures, the document recommended, should serve only as a guide and not as a determining factor in selecting students. The numerical figure, it explained, was merely to "provide a means of roughly sorting students in the order of preference," and "all final decisions should be checked against the individual record to be sure that points not adequately considered in the mathematical figure can be taken into account." In addition, the student's scholarship rating should weigh more in the consideration than personal factors. The latter category, the document observed, was flawed in that it was more susceptible to subjective and inaccurate measures; colleges generally attached greater importance to scholarly performance, and "giving first place to scholastic achievement is sound, is the common practice, [and the] one most likely to be acceptable to all concerned."[29]

Besides ranking students, the Council had to demonstrate "community acceptance" of nisei students. In its procedure dated July 24, 1942, the Council outlined one set of requirements for students held in assembly centers and another for those in the concentration camps. For those in assembly centers maintained by the Army-controlled WCCA, the Council required "a statement from some public official such as a public welfare agency, Mayor, Chief of Police, District Attorney, or other responsible town or county Peace Officer indicating that he sees no reason why Japanese American students should not be relocated in that community." For those in the concentration camps run by the civilian WRA, "no statement from the Mayor or public official is required." Rather, "a statement from some official from the receiving college or university is sufficient."[30]

A summary sheet accompanying a student application for a travel permit from the WCCA, dated July 30, 1942, provides an example of the end result of the Council's work. A telegram from the University of Wisconsin's graduate school indicated the student's acceptance, bank statements showed the student to have $1,274.06, a letter from Madison's district attorney and two women sponsors in Madison testified to community acceptance, and references from the student's undergraduate institution attested to her character. Fresno's superintendent of schools described the student as "a most estimable young woman," and the president of Fresno State Junior College wrote: "She has our complete confidence as to her loyalty, integrity, and high professional standards." And one of her former professors wrote that the student was "responsible, industrious, and honest. . . . [She] is the type of young, loyal American Japanese that it is a privilege to associate with and to know."[31]

Establishing the "loyalty" of nisei students was clearly a major hurdle, over and above the usual requirements of academic ability and financial capacity, for the student applicant and Council. But nisei students also faced the military's insistence that it approve the institutions at which those students could study. During the summer of 1942, there were many more qualified students and institutions willing to take those students than there were institutions cleared by the military. Robbins Barstow, the Council's director, wrote to the West Coast office's Conard in July 1942, "I think we must resign ourselves to a very slow and cumbersome process." The WRA, he explained, sought to expedite matters, but "their hands are tied just as much as ours are. The Army is endeavoring to devise some system of rating for the colleges under which we can operate. According to present indications," Barstow reported, "there will be a small list of institutions completely in the clear. Then the vast majority will be subject to individual clearances on specific requests covering definite student nominations." For the moment, he despaired, the Council had to settle for "trial and error methods as we get turned down again and again [by the military] from this or that institution." He concluded: "Now it is quite as heart-breaking for me to have to write this way as it must be for you to get this discouraging word, but we simply have to [be] realistic and face the fact and these facts are that the situation is beyond our control."[32]

Military clearance meant that an institution was not carrying on classified research or located within twenty-five miles of "important power installations, defense factories or railroad terminal facilities." Those Army criteria excluded nisei students from virtually all major research universities and institutions in urban areas. The Navy proscribed institutions where naval scientific research was being conducted and those with naval ROTC units. "While the Army's decision to rule out institutions within 25 miles of strategic locations excludes many of the more desirable urban universities," admitted the WRA's John H. Provinse, "I am hopeful that an appeal will broaden the list, and that permission to attend some of these institutions may be obtained, at least in the case of individuals whose loyalty can be established. For the present, however," he summed up the situation, "the criteria stated above should be used as a guide in making approaches to colleges and universities which may be interested to participate in the student relocation plan."[33]

Because few colleges and universities met the military's criteria for clearance and because the procedure took such a long time, few nisei students were actually placed in institutions when the fall 1942 school year began. In its progress report dated October 1, 1942, the Council's West Coast office had received 2,321 applications from nisei who wanted to attend college that fall. Of that total, 800 had completed folders, and 500 had been accepted by colleges but awaited their release. The Council helped 105 of the 500 accepted students, whereas the remainder, 395, had been accepted through the student's initiative and not that of the Council. Despite the acceptance of 500 nisei, at the time, a mere 147 colleges had been cleared by the military, and only 152 students left the detention camps and enrolled in college that fall.[34]

By December, however, the military had cleared 344 colleges, and there were 1,800 openings but an insufficient number of applicants to fill them. "Unfortunately," the brief report noted, "about two thirds of these offerings are for women, whereas two thirds of our applicants are men. Many of the remaining vacancies are in small denominational schools," the report continued. "Some are in colleges where the community has turned sour. Nevertheless it is true that there are openings waiting to be filled and students who may be persuaded to fill them." The task now was "not only do we have to sell students to colleges, but we have to sell colleges to students who never heard of them, — colleges like Haverford, Swarthmore, Kenyon, Rochester are sometimes as unfamiliar and unattractive as Shreiner, Simpson, Stephens, or Sterling."[35]

The Council's West Coast offices were buzzing with activity, especially as the deadlines for fall enrollment approached. Its San Francisco office showed in its December 15, 1942, personnel and financial report four working in general administration, five (two full-time, one half-time, and two temporaries) in the student records department, six in placement, two in financial aid, four in the permit department, one in a college information department, two filing and mail clerks, and eight (five full-time, two half-time, and one "occasional") in the stenographic pool. All received modest salaries, except for three volunteers who drew no salary from the Council. They administered, assembled student application folders, matched students with institutions, found financial aid, sought leave permits, provided general information, and typed, duplicated, filed, and mailed the volumes of reports and correspondences.[36]

In addition to its paid staff, the Council depended on a host of volunteers, like Margaret Cosgrave, the registrar at Fresno State College who gave up her summer to work on nisei student relocation. Born in Fresno, Cosgrave lived mainly among Whites, and knew no Japanese Americans during her formative years. She graduated from Stanford University in 1926, and returned to Fresno to work at the college. She became its registrar during the mid-1930s. Cosgrave was introduced to her nisei students' plight in 1942, when she, as registrar, was approached by several nisei who wanted to transfer from Fresno State to colleges outside the military exclusion zone. Also, the dean of women, Mary Baker, was a former missionary in Japan and spoke Japanese fluently. She knew many of the area's Japanese American families, and alerted her colleagues to the impending mass removal.

Cosgrave somehow learned of a meeting in Berkeley of concerned educators and others in the spring of 1942, and traveled there to attend the gathering. The group formed was the Student Relocation Committee, headed by Joseph Conard, but also the brainchild of a Mrs. Kingman of the YMCA. During the Committee's discussions about student placement involving application forms, transcripts, and the like, Cosgrave "realized," she said, that she "could be quite useful" because of her experience as a college registrar. That summer, during her vacation, she left Fresno for Berkeley to work in the Committee's office, by then renamed the Student Relocation Council, with other staffers and volunteers. The collection included well-meaning people, but many had little of the skills and training necessary to sort through student applications, figure grade point averages, and deliberate in the selection process. This was, Cosgrave recalled fondly, "a strange group of volunteers." Still, the assembly was a "friendly group" and the office was "bustling and enthusiastic." They knew they were engaged in a valuable and worthy project.

Cosgrave probably spoke for her fellow volunteers in that Berkeley and later San Francisco office when she identified the reason that animated her and this "strange group of volunteers" who gave up their vacations, summers, and weekends and who labored without salaries. "It needed doing," she said simply. "The whole reason for it

[the mass removal and detention] was so very wrong, and more people should have done it [the work of helping Japanese Americans]."
Others, she added, did help, like Marguerite Lopez of Fresno, a white
woman, who kept in touch with her Japanese American friends in
the detention camps and sent them needed items. Cosgrave confided,
almost lovingly, in remembering her labors on behalf of nisei students, "it was my first cause."[37]

A series of letters from Joseph Conard to Drake University's direc-
tor of admissions reveal some of the work of the West Coast office.
Letters from Dillon S. Myer, the WRA director who replaced Milton
S. Eisenhower in June 1942, and Robbins W. Barstow, director of the
Student Relocation Council, preceded Conard's application to Drake.
Those letters presumably lay the groundwork for the placement of
nisei students at Drake, and Conard's August 26, 1942, letter informed
Drake's admissions director of the process by which the nisei students
were selected. "After painstaking study and investigation," he
explained, "a sub-committee composed of experienced college and
university deans and admission officers is now making the recommendations to the colleges concerned." To place students, Conard
continued, institutions must first admit them and only then would
the federal government clear those institutions for nisei placement.
He thus submitted the names of three nisei students, two men and
one woman, who "rank in the highest ten percent on basis of scholastic performance and personal qualities" as determined by the West
Coast office. If they were accepted by Drake, Conard added, the university should provide someone "who would be willing to act as
confidential adviser and friend to the nominee."[38]

It appears that the Council's strategy was to present their highest
ranking students as the first applicants to a college or university to
secure that institution's admission of the nisei. With that approval,
the Council could seek the government's clearance of the institution
for more nisei students. In that way, the best and the brightest nisei
served to open the door for those less qualified (as deemed by the
Council). That became evident when Conard followed his initial letter to Drake with another, two days later. In this letter to the admissions director, Conard recommended seven more students whose
records were mixed when compared with the original group of nom-

inees. Although one student had already received her master's degree and had compiled an academic record of great distinction, one by his own accounts was a "C" student at a junior college, another was considered an "above average" student by the director of student aid at his university, and yet another attended a business college and was ranked "average, or above" in her personal qualities by her references.[39]

In March 1943, all of the Council's West Coast offices were closed, and the work of student relocation was centralized at a single office in Philadelphia. The Council changed its name to the National Japanese American Student Relocation Council to more accurately reflect its work, and some of the West Coast staff moved with their boxes of records to the new headquarters on the East Coast.

Equally important to the work of the West Coast offices that recruited, selected, and matched student with college were the efforts of committees in places that received those student (and other) relocatees. Chicago's Advisory Committee for Evacuees was established in July 1942 "to pave the way . . . for evacuees" by serving as a clearing center for information and services that were provided by various social agencies in the city.[40] At the organizational meeting of the committee, the American Friends Service Committee's Midwest branch was asked to head the coalition of churches, government agencies, private charities, the YMCA and YWCA, and several nisei volunteers. Those organizations and individuals agreed to carry on with their own work, with the Advisory Committee serving as a means by which to coordinate their efforts at solving "the problem of evacuees from the West Coast," including that of nisei students and "voluntary evacuees" already in Chicago, according to the minutes of the Advisory Committee's founding meeting.[41]

Although released from the WRA concentration camps, the "evacuees" remained under the military's "protective custody," but not under its care. For their needs, many Japanese Americans relied on the Advisory Committee's member services that included employment and finance, housing, personal counseling, social adjustment, civil rights, and student relocation. The Advisory Committee gave sustained and careful consideration to "community interpretation," or the monitoring and molding of public opinion regarding Japanese Americans, a student relocation priority as was identified from the start.[42]

By the end of September 1942, Chicago's Advisory Committee reported having helped sixty-eight nisei who faced problems of community approval, employment, housing, and government regulations, and asked for personal and educational counseling. Advisory Committee members, the report noted, gave "numerous speeches" to clubs, churches, and other community organizations in their task of "interpretation," and they distributed hundreds of pamphlets and bulletins on the plight of Japanese Americans. They also mailed "books, toys, and soap" to those held in several of the concentration camps.[43]

In February 1943, Margaret T. Morewood, with the assistance of Florence Scott, undertook a review of the first 402 students relocated to colleges and universities during the fall of 1942. A few of those students arrived on campus during the winter term of 1943. Using the Council's files, Morewood and Scott provided a profile of that first group. There were 269 men and 133 women among that group, clustered around the ages of eighteen to twenty-two. The vast majority of those students were already in college at the time of their removal from the West Coast: 25 percent were high school seniors; 21 percent were first-year college students; 19.5 percent, sophomores; 20 percent, juniors; and 3.25 percent, seniors. There were 34 graduate students, or 8 percent of the total.

Although nearly all (400 of 402) of the nisei students received some help from the National Student Relocation Council, the vast majority (315, or 78.5 percent) of this first group gained admittance to college through their own efforts. Besides their independence in negotiating the bureaucracy, those students possessed the necessary financial support to gain their release from the detention camps and attend college. The students' own cash in hand, in savings and checking accounts, was the principal source of their assets, along with the assets of their sponsors (parents, guardians, relatives, friends) and their annual incomes. Fully 35 percent aspired to vocations in engineering, commerce, and medicine, but majors in the social sciences, education, social welfare, nursing, and physical sciences were also popular. The next group of educational and career goals included business administration, agriculture, pharmacy, home economics, the ministry, music, dentistry, and law.

Most of that first group of 402 nisei students attended colleges in the Rocky Mountain and Midwest regions. The University of

Nebraska had the largest number with 46, followed by Washington University with 31, the University of Utah with 30, and the University of Denver with 26. The most popular colleges along the East Coast were Chesbrough Seminary in New York with 6 nisei students, Haverford College in Pennsylvania and Smith College in Massachusetts with 4 each, and Swarthmore College in Pennsylvania with 3. Most of those institutions were small liberal arts colleges, and many had religious affiliations. They also included vocational schools like the Barnes School of Commerce in Colorado, St. Mary's School of Nursing in Minnesota, and the Vogue School of Design. And while the vast majority of that first group of 402 students attended institutions with at least one other nisei, 53 went to campuses where they were the only relocated student. The latter were scattered in places like Baylor University in Texas, Colby College in Maine, Johnson Bible College in Tennessee, and St. Joseph's School of Nursing in Montana.

Many of this first group were among the elite of their generation. Besides their financial resources and their individual initiatives, they had a record of academic achievement. According to Morewood and Scott, they were "a very superior group scholastically, and the majority were Honor Students and held positions of honor, such as President of Class, or President of Student Body." One student held the "highest scholastic standing" in the senior class at a state university and won the gold medal award.

The war and its dislocations affected profoundly the course of those students' education and for some their career choice. Assuredly it forced them to transfer from their home institutions to campuses that were open to them, but for some it also compelled a rethinking of their future in postwar America. As a nisei student put it, his idea was "to keep the economic balance of the world right, so we can live peacefully," while another testified, "My goal seems tragically ironic now, but as an American citizen, of Japanese ancestry, it was to further good relationship between Japan and the U.S.A." Education, wrote yet another nisei, made her optimistic about the future. "Nothing could have affected me and led me toward a light as the American School. I saw young people expressing themselves honestly, eagerly and intelligently on international affairs. . . . Here I gained my belief in common man who takes part in his society. The State exists for the people, by the people, of the people. Man is able to take steps toward a better society in cooperation with others. He is far better than the people of the past. I began to believe things may push back a little, but on the whole there is progress."[44]

That progress evidenced in the lives of nisei students was gained, in large measure, through the determined and courageous efforts of the students themselves and of those who assisted them in taking those steps toward "a better society."

THREE

Exemplars

"THE WHITE-MAGIC OF RAPPORT between students and staff illuminates exchanged volumes of correspondence," Morewood and Scott's report of the first 402 nisei students observed. "It runs like a living flame through records. Evidence of a vital comradeship established is here. The staff has built up a security in the minds of students that students count on. As the Director's letter of February 6th, 1943, sent out to tell the students of moving plans, is addressed: 'Dear Fellow Worker' and advises that each student 'is an ambassador paving the way for others' so all through the relationship of staff and students a fellowship has been created."[1]

In truth, the letters exchanged between nisei students and the Council's staff, like Roy Nakata's letters to his family's friend, Alice Sinclair Dodge, revealed simultaneously aspects of the young authors' lives and the course of relationships driven by the winds of war. They also chronicle the suspense, anguish, and sometimes triumph that accompanied the student application process, a usual procedure but rendered unusual, with its own twists and turns, by the exigencies of dislocation and detention camps. For the nisei, student life tested resources and abilities, but also their will.

Jerry K. Aikawa, a first-year medical student at the University of California, sent queries to several medical schools during March and April 1942 in anticipation of the mass eviction from the West Coast. Of that group, only the University of Oklahoma responded. On May 7, Aikawa received a rejection notice from Oklahoma, and on May 11 he mailed queries to nineteen other medical schools, including Wake Forest College. In his letter to Wake Forest's registrar, Aikawa explained: "Due to the Army evacuation orders affecting even loyal American citizens of Japanese ancestry, I am unable to continue my education here [at the University of California]." Four days later, Herbert M. Vann, chair of the admissions committee at Wake Forest medical school, informed Aikawa that there were vacancies in the sophomore class, but cautioned him: "I shall be glad to receive all your credentials and to present your application to our admissions committee, but I am not at all certain as to their reaction in your case." The school's next term, Vann added, would begin on June 29.

Meanwhile, probably before receiving Vann's somewhat encouraging reply, Aikawa was removed to Stockton Assembly Center on May 18, and from Stockton Aikawa was taken to Rohwer Relocation Project, the WRA concentration camp in McGhee, Arkansas. By June 29 when Wake Forest's school term began, Aikawa had heard nothing from the college directly but learned from the University of California that Wake Forest had vacancies in its sophomore medical class for the term beginning in March 1943. No doubt anxious, Aikawa wrote Vann on September 19, reminding the admissions director of his earlier correspondence and asking if he might be admitted for the March term. "I am writing this," Aikawa pressed, "to ask if there are vacancies in the March class and also if the attitude in Winston-Salem would make it possible for me to attend school there."

On September 25, Vann responded to Aikawa's query and reported that he had met with his committee that day. "As you well understand," he wrote, "we have been most sympathetic from the start, and it has been our desire to work out plans for enrolling you in this School if possible." But, Vann explained, the college needed some assurance from the federal government that North Carolina was not in a restricted military zone, and "several letters" to the FBI and military authorities had only resulted in being passed from one agency to another. The college thus was unclear as to its status. "It has been suggested by my committee," continued Vann, "that we put the burden of furnishing us this information on you; therefore, if you have any circulars or bulletins of information on this matter, I think it will be well for you to forward them to me."

Aikawa consulted immediately with two members of the WRA staff

Young women in Amache, Colorado, concentration camp, fall 1942: Agnes Yamamoto Kawate (last on right) and her sister Lucy (middle). (Agnes Yamamoto Kawate)

Agnes Yamamoto Kawate (last row, first on left) and fellow canteen workers at Merced Assembly Center, California, 1942. (Agnes Yamamoto Kawate)

Agnes Yamamoto Kawate's
mother and father in Amache
concentration camp. (Agnes
Yamamoto Kawate)

Agnes Yamamoto Kawate,
school photograph, St. Mary's
College, winter 1942. (Agnes
Yamamoto Kawate)

Mr. and Mrs. Kanno (left), Kayo Asai Suzukida, and brother Sadaichi, Poston concentration camp, 1945. Suzukida returned to Poston to attend her mother's funeral. (Kayo Asai Suzukida)

Kayo Asai Suzukida at the Eastern Baptist Theological Seminary, Philadelphia, November 1943. (Kayo Asai Suzukida)

Nisei students and friends at Dakota Wesleyan University, Mitchell, South Dakota, 1944. The nisei students from left to right are Akira Yokomichi, William Marutani, and Min Yoshida. (Min Yoshida)

Mary Fujii Yasukawa (front left) and friends, Manchester College, North Manchester, Indiana. (Mary Fujii Yasukawa)

Graduation, Washington University, St. Louis, Missouri, June 1944: Setsuko Matsunaga, Gladys Ishida, Lillian Kubota (front row, left to right); Hiroshi Kesamoto, Shotaro Tsuruoka, Tsuyoshi Itano, George Matsumoto, Yoshio Matsumoto (back row, left to right). (Yoshio Matsumoto)

Yoshio Matsumoto at Washington University. (Yoshio Matsumoto)

Esther Suzuki and roommate Jean Bergquist show pictures of their fiances, Kirk Hall, Macalester College, St. Paul, Minnesota. (Esther Suzuki)

Esther Suzuki and friends Eunice (left) and Dorothy Mark (center) in front of the old library, Macalester College. (Esther Suzuki)

Alice Abe Matsumoto (left) and Yoshiko Uchida (right) in Philadelphia, summer 1944. Matsumoto attended Temple University. (Alice Abe Matsumoto)

Louise Seki Hoare and classmates on graduation day, Simmons College, Boston, June 15, 1945

"The Shortest Basketball Team in the Nation." This publicity photograph of
Kalamazoo College's 1944 men's varsity basketball team gained national attention: team captain Hazen Keyser (lower left, front row), Thomas Sugihara,
Louie Spitters, Paul Hiyama (upper left, back row), and Gus Birtsas. (Kalamazoo College Archives, with special thanks to Monica Scheliga Carnesi, assistant
reference librarian)

in the Rohwer camp, and they in turn referred his case to Joseph Conard of the Student Relocation Council. On November 11, Trudy King of the Council's permit department reported to Aikawa that the matter was well in hand and the military was considering the "routine clearance" for Wake Forest. "Now, although March is sometime away," King added, "we would like to start collecting all your documents so that there will be no delay in 1943." She then proceeded to list the requirements to obtain a student leave from the camp, including an official acceptance letter from the college and proof of finances. The professionalism in King's letter and the swath it cut through the dense bureacracy must have been exhilarating to Aikawa.

In a letter dated November 20, Wake Forest's medical school dean wrote to Aikawa: "The Admissions Committee of this medical school has approved your application for admission to the second-year class, entering March 22, 1943. This is to officially inform you of this action." But that acceptance was just another step toward the school door. He still needed his leave clearance from the FBI. Aikawa was granted his student leave on January 1, 1943, and two days later an excited Aikawa wrote to Vann: "The teletype report to this project from Washington, D.C., on January 1 informed me that I had been cleared by the F.B.I. so that I am now definitely able to attend medical school."

Aikawa's dependence on the kindness of others didn't end there. He needed housing, but also had to show that the Winston-Salem community would accept him as a Japanese American. The wife of a Wake Forest medical student, Mrs. J. T. McRae, wrote to Aikawa on January 18. McRae had entered medical school in June 1942, his wife explained, and they had been married in September. She worked on the hospital staff, and was willing to help Aikawa find a room. "We are sure that there will be no difficulty in finding living quarters," she reported to him. "Winston-Salem is not overcrowded." She had asked the Chamber of Commerce to send Aikawa literature on the city and surrounding area, McRae continued, and would soon send material on the college. "You will love this state," she closed. "It is beautiful— mountains in the distance, green rolling hills between, weather that peps us up. Welcome to our midst and more power to your medical career! We look forward to your friendship."

The next day, McRae wrote to Aikawa: "Even before I had finished a survey of the best possible living quarters near the school a special request came in today from one of my finest neighbors asking that she have the privilege of offering you a room in her home. She is Mrs. Whitfield Cobb, 2001 Elizabeth Avenue, whose son, Whitfield, is a member of the Friends religious denomination." Although it isn't clear in this set of letters, the Council commonly utilized its network of Friends to advise upon and secure housing and to undertake the work of "community interpretation," creating a welcoming atmosphere to receive nisei students. "Mrs. Cobb has several medical students in her home now," McRae continued. "She has told them that she is asking you to come and all of them are looking forward to your arrival. You will hear from her in a few days." McRae ended with the encouraging, "We are proud of your splendid scholastic record. Congratulations for past efforts and Godspeed for the future!"[2]

At times, while confined in camps, nisei students faced the uncertainty of having to select colleges from colorful brochures that made false claims. Unlike those who had freedom of movement, they couldn't undertake campus visits. Walter Funabiki, whose education at Stanford was interrupted by the military's mass evictions, wrote to the Student Relocation Council's Joseph Conard from his new "home" at Heart Mountain concentration camp in Wyoming in September 1942. "I would very much like to attend the Chicago Institute of Technology in Illinois," he informed Conard. "I would appreciate it very much if I may continue my studies there." A few days later, Funabiki sent Conard an addendum listing his third, fourth, and fifth choices after the Chicago Institute of Technology. "Can you tell me how my chances are?" he inquired. "I confess that I am very anxious to continue my school[ing]."

While waiting for word on admissions, Funabiki worked for about a month outside the Heart Mountain camp harvesting sugar beets on nearby farms. "Financing my education through sugar beet topping was very discouraging," he reported to Council staff member Virginia Scardigli. "What little I managed to earn was dropped in a little Wyoming town in exchange for gifts to my folks from the outside civilization. So you see here I am again without a very bright outlook financially except for what I had earned previously from threshing beans here in Cody." In any case, he added, "the present snowfall has curtailed my mercenary hopes for the year."

Having struggled to earn money for his education, Funabiki, the aspiring engineer, vented some of his frustration over the government's requirement that prospective students must have the necessary financial resources before gaining release from the camp. "But why can't students who are able and had experience in earning their own way through school leave the camp and do so?" he asked. "It is much better to leave camp now and face our problems—to fail or to succeed; that doesn't matter much, if we know that we tried and enjoyed doing so. Life in camp is not exactly encouraging for those who wish to continue their education for whatever price they have to pay," he declared. And, he added to Scardigli, "please forgive me if I seem selfish when I say that my hopes were brightened by your words 'perhaps we can work something out for you.'"

On November 17, 1942, Funabiki wrote to Scardigli: "I received your encouraging letter just before dinner yesterday, and if you should ask me what I ate, I would have no answer because I was reading your letter for the fourth or fifth time." He paused to explain: "Please excuse me for rushing through the introductory phase of this letter for I am rather excited about answering all your questions." After reporting his interest in the Milwaukee School of Engineering, Funabiki noted that "the subject of my finance is still rather discouraging." Because of the detention, he wrote, his father's income was "very limited," and all he had saved thus far was $100 to $150, the sum total of his "treasury" upon which depended his "educational ambition." But, he noted, "I wish to thank you again for your encouraging letters. I hope, selfishly, that I receive more of them."

The Milwaukee School of Engineering accepted Funabiki's application for the term beginning January 2, 1943. "Do you think I could possibly make the Winter quarter?" Funabiki asked Scardigli. "If not is there a possibility of going there and working until the Spring quarter?" Funabiki was clearly eager. On January 4 and still in the Heart Mountain camp, Funabiki wished Scardigli a peaceful new year and predicted optimistically, "I have a hunch this year is starting off on its right foot for me." Although the correspondence is a bit vague, it appears that a Dr. Smith helped secure a grant toward Funabiki's education. "I was surprised and glad to hear about Dr. Smith," Funabiki wrote. "We knew him quite well through his swell work in the Methodist Church. I hate to take advantage of his unselfish nature but please tell him that I will repay him somewhere, somehow, for his kind efforts." And on a personal note to Scardigli, Funabiki asked: "Is San Francisco still in fog? The Relocation Council ought to move into Santa Clara valley where it's really sunny," he suggested.

On the eve of his departure from Heart Mountain, Funabiki wrote to Scardigli: "In a few days I hope to embark on an entirely new experience. I feel certain that all will be my profit." The nisei should wean themselves away from the issei, he advised, "it's time that we walk along by ourselves. I realize the difficulties I may face but I believe that a life without any problems isn't worth living." And, he added, "some day I know that I am going to repay you for your wonderful help. I know that it may take a long time but I have hope, because I am also determined to live a long life."

"I arrived in Milwaukee Wednesday morning at 8:30 A.M.," Funabiki reported to Scardigli on March 28, 1943. "I was taken to the school right after and was introduced to Mr. Oscar Werwath, the president," who, Funabiki noted with some consternation, asked him for his tuition money. "About the second thing he mentioned after saying hello was my tuition fee," recalled Funabiki. "Mentioning it was all right but he just about demanded it. Little bewildered and tired from the trip I paid him $110." Later, after having met and talked with several other nisei students already at the Milwaukee school, Funabiki learned that they all shared the same view of the school: "the school has a very private and mercenary atmosphere which is noticeable on the first day." After having paid their tuition, the nisei students found that a single building constituted the school's entirety "with little and poor equipment and laboratory," no gymnasium, and "a small room with two tables for the library." Worst of all, there were few instructors and virtually no choice in selecting a course of study.

"Please don't think we are complaining without reasons or are crying for help," Funabiki implored Scardigli. "Some of the students are going to remain mainly because they had already paid their tuition and started in some courses. I am still troubled and undecided but in the meantime I am trying to locate another college or university. If you know of any which are open please let me know." And, he urged the Council's staff member, "please discourage any other potential students of this school, for I am almost sure that they will feel disappointed in coming here."

Funabiki ultimately decided to withdraw from the school and asked for a tuition refund. After two weeks, the school finally returned his tuition and that of two other nisei, but kept $25, which, the school maintained, was their registration fee. Three other nisei students, according to Funabiki, had asked for refunds and were awaiting a ruling on their request. "Most of the students are planning to work until they find another school," he continued. "I have also decided to work until I can enter some school for the summer session." Funabiki's letters updated the Council on his whereabouts and status, because, as he recognized, "even though I am now out of camp I must still ask for your help in selecting a school."

On July 30, 1943, Funabiki could report at last that he was "enrolled and busy with my studies again" in Columbia, Missouri. He had a nice room for $1 a week, was eating at the "Three Squares Coop," and held a job in the registrar's office for an hourly wage of 35 cents. The students, teachers, and townspeople were all "very friendly and helpful," noted Funabiki, "so I am enjoying my stay here quite a bit." By September of that year, Funabiki could happily report to the Council's Trudy King, "I'm still here." He had secured a job as a research assistant in the engineering department, and earned extra money working as a "bus boy" in the cafeteria at nearby Stephens College. "Believe me," Funabiki confessed to King, "I never saw so many dishes—and girls! Just between you and me, I sometimes find it difficult to keep from dropping a few dishes when some beautiful Stephens students walk by."[3]

For some students like Wiley Higuchi, making enough money for their education was "seemingly hopeless." After meeting with a counselor in Santa Anita Assembly Center, Higuchi wrote to the Student Relocation Council's Joseph Conard on August 25, 1942. He noted how encouraging it was, under the present circumstances, to learn about the Council and its "unselfish and benevolent undertaking." "Although many of we Nisei will not be able to complete our college education," Higuchi predicted, "it is compensation in itself to know that there are so many of you Caucasion [*sic*] fellow-Americans who are interested in the future of our small minority." He had worked to support his mother since his father's death in 1934, Higuchi recalled to Conard, and had completed the sophomore year of his pre-legal studies at the University of California, Los Angeles, when the mass removals ended his education. Higuchi asked the Council for information about schools that were open to the nisei and about the possibilities of receiving financial aid.

Nearly a year later, Higuchi was still in a detention camp, having been taken from Santa Anita to the WRA camp at Gila River, Arizona. "It seems that it takes an awfully long time for leave clearances of students to come through," he exclaimed to the Relocation Council's Howard K. Beale in May 1943. "I filled out my leave clearance about a month ago, but nothing has come of it as yet." Besides his anxiety over getting permission to leave the camp, Higuchi worried about saving enough money to continue his education. "I would like to apply for admission to Loyola University in Chicago," he told Beale, "however, I may lack funds." He worked at the camp's camouflage net factory and managed to save $100, but the lint and dye from the fabric caused a severe skin rash among the workers and hence the factory was closed. His total savings of $450 would barely cover two semesters at Loyola, Higuchi figured, but he expected to work part-time. "If you think I should have more cash available before I go out to school, are there any funds in the Council's possession which are available for persons in my position?" he asked Beale. And, he closed: "I have the Application for Admission to Loyola in my possession and filled out. I shall be very anxiously awaiting your reply."

Higuchi made it to Chicago at the end of June 1943, and found a room in a hostel. "Things here are not what I expected and I am still hesitating to send my formal application into Loyola," he reported to the Council's Woodruff J. Emlen. "I will let you know as soon as I do, though." About a month later, Higuchi wrote to Emlen that he now planned to bring his mother from the concentration camp to join him in Chicago. "Under these circumstances," he explained, "the only way out for me in order to continue my education, which I am determined to complete no matter what happens, is to work a forty hour week and go to night school." So instead of going to Loyola, Higuchi picked De Paul University, which had "an excellent night school course where I could complete my pre-legal and legal work," he explained. "My first objective, however, is to get my mother out of the WRA center and back to normal living."

De Paul, Higuchi discovered, was willing to consider him for admission to its law school if he could show the completion of an associate of arts degree from UCLA. Upon inquiring, he found that he was just two units short of the degree. His having taught a fifth-grade class in the Gila River camp would have earned him nine units of credit from Tempe State Teacher's College in Arizona, but he had failed to ask for those units before he began teaching and thus didn't qualify to receive the credits. To complete his associate degree, Higuchi took six hours of college work for a semester while working to support himself.

He still planned to apply to De Paul's law school after that, Higuchi informed the Council's Trudy King, despite his uncertain prospects. "Some acquaintances want to discourage me from pursuing a legal career," he confided to King. "They contend that since Americans of Japanese ancestry are scattering all over the country, there will [be] little or no opportunity for private practice. What they say may be true, but my contention is that there is a greater service to be rendered to minority groups and to the United States as a democratic nation through the study and understanding of the laws and legal practices of the country."

"Final exams were over this week and I made my application to the School of Law," Higuchi exulted in a letter to the Council's Betty Emlen on December 16, 1943. Financing his education still concerned him, and could the Council extend to him some financial aid? he asked. The aid would allow him less work and more study time, and law school "requires a tremendous amount of reading and briefing cases as you realize," he reminded Emlen. But he also added thoughtfully, "I realize there are many Nisei in the same predicament." Part-time work could sustain him, he concluded, "but whatever help I can get will mean I can put more time into getting the most out of my studies."

On January 7, 1944, Higuchi wrote with obvious excitement to Betty Emlen: "At last! The good news came today. I received notice today that I was accepted by the De Paul University School of Law." He immediately went to the school, and on the elevator met one of the professors. "He was very friendly and we chated [*sic*] until I parted from him near the subway station," Higuchi told Emlen. "I really think I am going to like De Paul." And, he added, "thanks a million for all you and your associates have done for me up to now." Besides advising and encouraging Higuchi, the Council's staff had helped him secure transcripts and letters of recommendation and was consider-

ing his application for a tuition scholarship. "I shall be anxiously awaiting your next letter," Higuchi informed Emlen.

"Well, here I am struggling along in my first semester in Law
School," Higuchi reported in April 1944. He had been granted a $200
scholarship from the Presbyterian Board, arranged through the Relocation Council, and informed the Council, "I am very deeply grate-
full [*sic*] to all of you. To show my appreciation, I am trying to do
my best work." He had a flexible work schedule, he wrote Betty Emlen,
and so things were "working out pretty well. I get out of school at
twelve and I get to work about twelve thirty. When I get behind in
my case briefing, I go home instead and catch up. Everything has
worked out nicely for me so far, thanks to the Council." A few months
later, Higuchi found work during the week, from 5:30 to 8:30 P.M.,
in the university's college of commerce, earning $2 a night. On Sat-
urdays, he worked as a clerk in the Stevens Hotel, the "world's largest,"
he noted with pride. For his eight hours there, he earned $5.60.

By August, Higuchi had settled into life as a De Paul law student.
He had thought about transferring to the University of Minnesota,
he wrote Betty Emlen, "but I have such a good set-up as far as earning my current expenses and having time to study that I believe it
would be foolish to change." He also liked living in Chicago.
"Although work and law keeps me pretty busy," he admitted, "I try
to get down to the beach on Sundays when it's warm enough. Our
apartment is about a half mile from lake Michigan so it is very con-
venient." And he had a sense about his future. He planned to attend
law school as a day student for a full year, and complete his law degree
in his final year by working during the day in a law office and attending classes at night for three semesters. "That would mean I might
graduate in [the] summer of '46," he explained to Emlen. And, he
reported, "after nearly two semesters of law, I am beginning to feel
a little like a lawyer."[4]

But at times, individual determination and the aid of others were
not enough. Patriarchal attitudes and sexism intervened in the education of nisei women. Many, taught that their foremost responsibility was to stay home and care for their parents, were unable to pursue
an education. A nisei woman who wanted to become a teacher told
of her dilemma: "Mother and father do not want me to go out. However, I want to go so very much that sometimes I feel that I'd go even

if they disowned me. What shall I do? I realize the hard living conditions outside but I think I can take it."⁵

Another nisei woman described her predicament and plight in August 1942. "You probably have much more serious problems to occupy your time," she began deferentially to the Council, "but to me, my indefinite decision has caused me much worry and unhappiness." From her Tule Lake concentration camp barracks, she had applied for a school leave, "but like a hundred others received a letter telling me to be patient and wait." She couldn't wait, however, because her mother "doesn't see that I'm making any headway towards attending a school and has decided that I should get married instead." And her intended, "the fella," she reported, had also given her an ultimatum: "school or marriage."

Her predicament, she wrote, was all the more frustrating because her brother had received a positive response to his student application. A similar result, she was sure, would change her mother's mind and allow her to attend college. As far as she herself was concerned, "marriage would definitely be secondary if I was assured of going to school. Mother thinks I can have both, but in this particular situation it's an impossibility." Because of her circumstance, she had become "unhappy and ungraciously snappy." She would gladly supply any information that was needed to gain her release, but "in the meantime I shall be patiently waiting for an answer."⁶

Yet another nisei woman's family situation and her assigned role determined her response to the Council's offer of a scholarship to attend Smith College. Held at the Santa Anita detention camp, the woman testified: "To be able to go to Smith College is an opportunity which exceeds my wildest hopes." That dream, however, had to be deferred. "My father has just returned from the North Dakota Concentration Camp," she explained, "without seeing my sister who left the assembly center a week before to join her fiance. My mother is not feeling very well, and relocation is scheduled to start in October. I feel responsible for my parents and family in this trying period of confusion, and I must see them through in the adjustment period at the Relocation Center." Her decision to decline the scholarship offer, she confided, affected her deeply: "It hurts me harder than you can imagine to let this wonderful opportunity go, but I am sure that the recipient of this award will be a worthy one." After her family's move to a WRA concentration camp, she hoped to be considered for another offer, she requested of the Council, but only after her parents had resettled and "feel less bewildered if I left."[7]

The circumstances created by the concentration camps and the uncertainties of a future in postwar America wore upon nisei women in ways particular to their gender. Jeanne Mori reported her desire to pursue a religious education degree, but "I have a family and community responsibility," she explained, "so I am afraid I will not be able to leave. . . . I believe I shall be of better use if I remain with my family and people for the duration." And Mabel Sugiyama thanked the Student Relocation Council "from the bottom of my heart" for its efforts on her behalf, but, she reported, "my mother does not and will not let me leave to go to school . . . [for] she wants the family together as much as possible." At Tule Lake and separated from her father, who was being held in a Department of Justice camp in New Mexico, Sugiyama's mother wished to have them join him at the Lordsburg camp. After the war, Sugiyama speculated, her father would likely be deported to Japan and thus there would be another family move. The "uncertainty of our fate," explained Sugiyama, was a key factor in her decision to decline a college offer. But there was more. "If I were a boy," Sugiyama revealed, "this wouldn't matter too much because then my mother would not worry as much but being a girl all alone in a world which is bound to be filled with prejudices and discriminations, I feel I would rather stay with my mother."[8]

Mary Tanaka, as a high school student, dreamed of attending Smith College. "I used to read *Mademoiselle* magazine and I decided [a] long time ago, when I was in high school or junior high school that I was going to go to Smith College," she remembered. "It always sounded the most interesting." But when she graduated from the high school in Manzanar concentration camp in 1943, Tanaka had to delay her college career for her filial duties. Her two brothers had left the camp, one to finish his degree in architecture at Yale and the other to volunteer for the army reserve; and her father was being held in a Department of Justice camp in Montana, and later in New Mexico. Because of those circumstances and her assigned daughterly role, Tanaka felt responsible for the care of her mother and remained with her in Manzanar. But when the teenager learned that her father had been granted a second hearing at the Santa Fe camp in 1944, Tanaka seized the opportunity to gain his release so he could rejoin the family in Manzanar and thereby free her to pursue her college education. "I assembled a lot of documentary affidavits from administrative people from Manzanar and from family friends and other Japanese and non-Japanese," recalled Tanaka. "Even the director of Manzanar wrote an affidavit saying how nice his children were. . . . I got clearance to go to Santa Fe to attend the hearing. At the end of the hearing, the head of the hearing board said, 'Don't worry little girl, you'll be able to go to school.'" In the fall of 1944, Tanaka's father was released from Santa Fe to rejoin his family in Manzanar, and in February of the following year Mary Tanaka entered Wheaton College in Norton, Massachusetts.[9]

Some issei parents, contrary to the patriarchal ideal, encouraged their daughters' education and careers outside the home. "Tomae was the first feminist to cross my path," wrote Esther Suzuki of her mother Tomae Tamaki Torii. "Having a teaching certificate, she was a firm believer in education. Having had a good education herself, she valued this for her three daughters. She was a realist also and did not believe that a woman's role was just to make a 'good marriage' by marrying a wealthy man and being supported for her lifetime." Indeed, Tomae enrolled in the Minnesota Literacy Program after twenty-six years of work as a seamstress, and thereby became the oldest student in the state. Suzuki's father, Tokichi Torii, also valued education for his daughters. "Education has been the single most important factor stressed by our parents," Suzuki attested. "From the day that my father escorted me to the front of the kindergarten class and entrusted me to the teacher with these words, 'Please, you teachum her English,' I have been on a one-track course."[10]

At his grandmother's funeral in 1989, Tomae's grandchild eulogized her: "Grandma was very progressive in her time," declared Jay Kirihara. "Grandma instilled in her three daughters the importance of self-reliance and independence. This is why she encouraged Esther, Eunice and Lucy to pursue their college education and careers. She was proud of what her daughters have achieved. Grandma saw her vision realized."

In support of their daughters' education, Esther Suzuki recalled, parents in the detention camps, cut off from their previous sources of income, engaged in extraordinary labor. Her mother worked late at night stringing tiny beads onto leather moccasins for a man who paid five cents apiece and sold the moccasins as handcrafted American Indian souvenirs. "The hours that went into the countless tiny moccasin stitches would be like counting the grains of sand in the desert," Suzuki observed of her mother's labor of love. Another mother played the piano in camp every chance she got to pay for her daughter's expensive private school tuition. Those acts of motherly devotion and sacrifice must have uplifted and at the same time weighed heavily on the spirits of their nisei daughters.

Suzuki's family—her mother, father, and two sisters—were forcibly evicted from their Portland, Oregon, home and placed in a detention camp on May 5, 1942. She was not allowed to leave the camp the following month to attend her high school graduation, and instead received her diploma in the mail. At first, she remembered, the days in that Portland detention center "dragged endlessly." "Then the pieces of a great cosmic puzzle began to miraculously fit together," she wrote, when she heard about the student relocation program. With a scholarship from the Relocation Council and a letter of acceptance from Charles J. Turck, the president of Macalester College in Minnesota, sixteen-year-old Esther Suzuki left the camp to pursue her college education. "For my first assignment in freshman speech class," Suzuki recalled, "I began by declaring, 'The happiest day of my life was the day I left for college.' But suddenly I remembered my father, mother and two sisters standing on the other side of the barbed wire fence in Oregon, waving goodbye, smiling bravely through their tears. I broke down and couldn't continue."

Suzuki observed that she learned about "human kindness and concern for others" during her years at Macalester. Those lessons were imparted by those who made her feel at home in Minnesota, far away from her family. Her faculty adviser, Milton McLean, "held open house," Suzuki recalled, "and all students were welcome to join his family in a light supper and fellowship." And when she learned that her family had contracted food poisoning and began crying, Mary Gwen Owen, a drama professor, bought her an ice cream cone to comfort her because, she said, no one could possibly eat ice cream and cry at the same time. Margaret Doty, the dean of women, gave her free tickets to the symphony, and Suzuki's fellow students invited her to their homes during the holidays. A friend's mother offered to wash

Suzuki's clothes, and yet another baked for her large oatmeal cookies which "smelled like the homemade soap she used" because they
were packed in a laundry box, but, admitted Suzuki, "I ate them with
relish." "It will take the rest of my life to pay back into the vast well
of human kindness that I found at Macalester," Suzuki concluded.[11]

Despite such instances of kindness, nisei women students still con-
fronted barriers that restricted their opportunities. Their choice of
careers was certainly circumscribed by racism, like nisei men, but also
by patriarchal attitudes unlike men. In 1943, the Student Relocation
Council undertook a survey of the fields of study of 3,029 nisei men
and women as shown on their applications to college. Of the 1,160
women, 263 chose nursing as their field of study, whereas only 3 men
did. And while 157 of the total 1,869 men chose chemistry, a mere 15
women selected that field. Likewise, 114 women chose general business, while only 35 men selected that field, and 138 men chose electrical engineering but no woman did. Majors and hence careers were
clearly gendered. The five most popular fields of study for women
were nursing, general business, dietetics, music, and sociology/anthro-
pology; and for men, chemistry, electrical engineering, mechanical
engineering, premedical, and agriculture.[12] A study of 1,000 nisei students during the war lists health, education, social work, business,
and home economics as the top five occupational choices of women;
and engineering, health, business, science, and agriculture as the top
choices of men.[13] "Business" for women frequently meant secretarial training, whereas for men, it implied another career track. Likewise, for men the choice of a "health" career generally meant studying
to become a physician, while for women it meant studying to become
a nurse.

Upon hearing that the *American Journal of Nursing* was planning
an article on nisei student nurses, Woodruff J. Emlen of the Student
Relocation Council wrote to the editor of the *Journal* to offer the
Council's assistance with the essay. As of August 1943, Emlen
informed the editor, 84 nisei women had been accepted into 24
schools of nursing, and there were 371 nisei women applicants for
nurse's training.[14] "We are anxious to publish a short article (about
500 words) in our October issue, which will go to press shortly,"
replied the *Journal*'s associate editor, "and I need a little more information from you. I also hope to write to one or two directors of nurs-

ing in schools where we know there are Japanese students for some of their impressions of the experience."[15] Emlen guided the article's author by answering the associate editor's questions, supplying her with the names of persons to contact, and suggesting editorial changes in the draft.[16]

Entitled "The Problem of Student Nurses of Japanese Ancestry," the article posed "the problem" of nisei women nursing students whose educations were cut short by the mass removals. Even with government permission, the author noted, the nisei "encounter resistance not met by ordinary university students." In contrast, "the girls want to be normal, they want to prove to the world that they are loyal, everyday Americans. Their right to an American citizen's opportunity cannot be denied." The author outlined the work of the Student Relocation Council, reported that schools with nisei students had "no unusual difficulties," and advanced the notion that nisei students "may well have a conciliatory influence in the Orient and throughout the world." Still, the author retreated, "it is not the function of this magazine to urge upon schools of nursing the course they are to take on this matter. It *is* the function of this magazine to place the facts before its readers and to urge careful, unbiased, and imaginative study of the situation . . . to the end that a solution may be found for loyal American girls whose ancestors happen to have been Japanese."[17]

Besides strikingly different choices of majors and careers, nisei women and men perceived contrasting problems as students. "My family did not approve of my 'striking out alone'" was the foremost problem confronting women, and their chief concerns included worrying over their families' financial situation, wanting to attend Buddhist church while in college, and clashing with their parents over concepts of good behavior. Men, on the other hand, chafed at college regulations that discriminated against the nisei, worried over future employment discrimination, and noticed racial discrimination in the Christian churches. Whereas a man saw racism as his principal problem, a women, the researcher observed, was more closely bound to the family, "causing her greater worry about the family finances . . . and greater conflict in choice of cultural standards."[18]

Student life was as varied as the problems and pleasures of nisei women and men and the hundreds of colleges and universities they attended throughout parts of the country that were open to them.

Constance Murayama was one of several nisei women who made it to Smith College in Northampton, Massachusetts. She described the joys of student life at Smith to Trudy King of the Student Relocation Council in a letter dated July 8, 1943. "It's just been wonderful in New England," Murayama, the Californian, exclaimed. "It's really a shock to find the weather travelling in cycles; in the autumn the leaves fall, in the winter it snows, and in the spring you want to go out and pound yourself on the chest and give Tarzan yells. Remarkable." In San Francisco, she remembered, everyone took the weather for granted, "but here, you're nice to it, or it bites back."

"Smith is really wonderful," Murayama declared emphatically. Perhaps in contrast to the University of California, Berkeley, where she was a student before the detention camps, Murayama was surprised to find that the professors "actually get to know you" and call you by name. "You meet them at teas and they talk to you. They announce their office hours, and they keep them. They apologize when they keep you, a mere student, waiting. It took a considerable time to accustom myself to all this." The course work was intense, "it was all giddily frenzied, and I loved it," and the school year zipped right along. Her liberal education also featured "some business training" to obtain skills for jobs that were open to her. Murayama, however, held higher ambitions than the socially prescribed roles assigned to her gender. "Of course," she wrote of her business training, "we [Murayama and her nisei friend, Helen] don't want to pound typewriters for a living, but then that training never is a waste of time."

Besides the change in seasons and her school work, Murayama enjoyed her living situation. She lived with a Smith professor of English and his wife, "one of the nicest families in the world." Both husband and wife, she noted, were "tremendously interested in the camps and were instrumental in organizing a benefit party for the schools there. It astonished me how well informed they were about IT all." Northampton was "really grand," she observed. The postman smiled at her, the soda-fountain woman engaged her in conversation, and the women along her street always greeted her in the morning. "It was an uplift to have total strangers so nice to us," she admitted, especially when compared with her "home" in a concentration camp: "I was agonizingly home-sick but when I thought that 'home' equalled camp, it's surprising how fast the nostalgia evaporated."

An incident involving a Mrs. Ichiyasu, nonetheless, served to remind Murayama of her wartime situation. Mrs. Ichiyasu, she wrote, was "hauled to the police station when some alert-fifth-columnist saw her sketching a bridge. She was unperturbed about it, though," reported Murayama. An alert Northampton citizen, no doubt, suspected Mrs. Ichiyasu's motives for her artwork. "She stuck to trees after that," Murayama noted of Mrs. Ichiyasu.[19]

Haruko Morita described the excitement of settling into student life at Phillips University in Enid, Oklahoma. "Although I came in at 11 o'clock at night," Morita wrote to the Council's Trudy King, "there were two carloads of Phillipians to meet me at the station when my train pulled in. From there on the students just took things over for me." They collected her bags and took her to the Barnes House, where she roomed with a different woman student each night for five nights until she could find a place to stay. "The girls did everything to make me feel at home, even offering to let me use their personal belongings," Morita exclaimed. Her first morning in Enid, Morita ate breakfast with the university's president and his family. "This was the first time in about a year and a half that I had sat in a dining room at a beautifully set table for breakfast," she noted with delight. A history professor and his wife offered Morita lodging in their home, and Mrs. Wellman, her host, treated her like a daughter. "I lost my mother when I was 12 years old," reflected Morita, "but I don't think my own mother could mother me anymore than Mrs. Wellman."

Morita attended the Big Little Sister Party, a faculty reception, receptions for new students, and a picnic held at Red Hill near the university's lake. The rural sociology class organized a hamburger fry at a local ranch. "We really had lots of fun," Morita admitted, "though we didn't learn much about rural sociology from our fry." "The friendly spirit of the Phillip Student is something you'll have to come down to see for yourself," she wrote to King. "I can't tell you how happy I am to be back in school again, especially at Phillips." And, she added, "I really think I am very fortunate to be a student at Phillips University."[20]

Student life could also be a grind, and sometimes the weather tried the very souls and constitutions of students from the sunbelt. "It's been snowing since Wednesday and I'm told it's still autumn!" Kazuko Nakamura exclaimed in her letter to Trudy King dated

November 13, 1943. "Holy smokes, it seems flannel underwear, wool slips, fur-lined gloves, woolen slacks, sweaters, and any other warm clothing are in order or I'll be a solid cake of ice before December gets underway," she declared of fall in Syracuse, New York. Seeing her first snow was "quite an experience," Nakamura recalled, and her "wild yelling and running around" must have seemed to others that she had "finally lost her mind." "What a spectacle—what an experience!" she wrote of watching snowflakes dance in the wind.

"The fall semester is practically over and final examinations are only 3 weeks away—and things are becoming pretty bad," Nakamura reported to King. "Especially with a term paper to write and three novels to read for English lit., besides catching up on Chemistry, Bacteriology and Mycology." She and her friend Ruth, Nakamura confessed, were procrastinators. "We leave everything for the night before the exam, or the morning of the exam." "Must tell you of some of the courses I'm suffering thru this term," she continued. Chemistry was "wearing me out" with its formulas and equations, advanced bacteriology was "highly elementary," mycology was "terribly dry and up in the fog," her German professor was "an adorable antique," and English literature gave her "a pain in the neck."

Nakamura glanced out her window as she wrote the letter, and excitedly declared: "Jeepers, it's snowing outside now (1:30 A.M.), and the snow is piling up! Holy mackeral—it's incredible. The ground is completely white. Looks as if we were in the middle of the desert. Br-rr! This coal rationing is terrific, how will I ever live through this cold!" The novelty of snow had not yet worn thin with that nisei student.[21]

Like Nakamura, Mary Ogi was fascinated with the change of seasons and the prospect of snow. "I'm still anxiously awaiting the snows—it's really going to be my biggest thrill I know," she wrote in October 1942 from Denver, but added, "that is, besides the news that I will be able to visit my family in Topaz, Utah, during Xmas vacation." Prominent in the letters of the first group of nisei student relocatees during the fall of 1942 were the physical and social settings of their new environments. They were often framed as a journey, from camp to college, and written as a travel account, a venture to novel climes and peoples. For many, the event was their first breach of California's or the West Coast's borders.

Describing her train ride to Denver, Mary Ogi remembered her excitement. "I wasn't going to miss a thing—this was my first trip out of state and last time in California for who knows how long," she wrote. The train ride for Ruth Hide Dohi was enjoyable, especially when she realized that she was leaving the confinement of a concentration camp. "The train trip across the country was most stimulating and welcome after such a severely restricted life," she observed. "Also it was quite soothing in effect; for once, I was a passive spectator outside of the moving scene, instead of being one of the surging multitudes embroiled in the constant churn of camp life." That "moving scene" outside the train's window, as Mary Ogi discovered, could also dull the senses. Of the "barren lands of Nevada and the sagebrush and salt beds of Utah," Ogi exclaimed, "my goodness, but it was monotonous—telephone poles and a blade of grass here and there. What did we do to deserve this!"

But once in the better watered and green slopes and valleys of the Rockies, Ogi's lungs took in the fresh mountain air and she perked up again. "How different Colorado was!" she wrote of its contrasts with the deserts. "After Nevada and Utah, Colorado was heaven-sent, with its red mountains, golden trees, and such *fresh air!*" And, she added about living in Denver, "I feel more alert now—maybe it's the Colorado air and water. I barely touched the water at Tanforan [assembly center in the Bay Area]. Now I am drinking it by the gallons."

Ruth Hide Dohi described Swarthmore, Pennsylvania, in November 1942. "Yes, the fall leaves were quite lovely here, and the countryside was most captivating and picturesque to my unaccustomed eye. Now that the leaves have fallen, the gaunt tall grandeur of the elm and maple and birch is most impressive. The houses, the slates on roof and walk are unique; the many, many unassuming factories, the quiet-flowing rivers, the green hills, the empty woods, the staid yet energetic atmosphere, the language, the temperament, and the people—all so very interesting and charming. I was very much thrilled to be in the East!" California, Dohi noted, was "very fine," but the Northeast was also "a wonderful place to be; though so different from home . . . it has so much to offer in richness of experiences and opportunities."[22]

With few exceptions, nisei students found warm and receptive communities and campuses in which to live and study. That, after all, was one of the criteria used in selecting the colleges and universities. Anomalous, thus, was Moscow, Idaho. Dubbed "the retreat from Moscow," six nisei students, three women and three men, who were admitted to the University of Idaho in the spring of 1942 had their acceptances canceled when "a small group of local roughnecks," according to the *Idaho Argonaut,* demanded their expulsion from town. Because of the threat of violence, the sheriff apparently placed two of the nisei women students in protective custody in the town's jail. "I feel very young and lost for once in my life," wrote one of those nisei from her jail cell. "Some of the townspeople are up in arms for our coming," she explained, "and are threatening mob violence. . . . The jailer was talking to someone over the telephone, and said that he is afraid that a mob will come to lynch us tonight. . . . Please write. I'm scared."[23]

By week's end, the students had been transported to another state. "Six American citizens were forced to leave their home city of Seattle last week," editorialized the April 23, 1942, *Idaho Argonaut.* "The reason was purely legitimate. The area had been declared a miliary zone and those students were of Japanese ancestry. Last night these same six American citizens were forced to leave their homes of one week in Moscow, but the reason was not military. It was a combination of political haymaking and the threat of violence by a small group of local roughnecks that forced this evacuation. . . . So six homesick kids, three boys and three girls, became the pawns in a political game and the live targets for jingoistic patriotism." The editorial went on to speculate that students must be shocked to learn that "here in a university town—where of all places objectivity, liberalism, and cool thinking should prevail—such ugly, violent, racial antagonism should flare up. When people begin thinking in terms of race, they are borrowing from the handbook of fascist leaders."[24]

In Parkville, Missouri, "the battle of Parkville" began when the mayor, Herbert A. Dyer, declared, according to the *St. Louis Star Times,* "that young men with enemy names should not be allowed the freedom of the town." He was supported in his opposition to the entrance of nisei students at Park College by the American Legion and American War Mothers. Dyer threatened court action if the college refused to expel from the town the three nisei students by September 1, 1942. According to the paper, Arthur Kamitsuka, one of the three, was studying for the ministry and had a brother serving in the U.S. Army; Henry

Masuda was vice president of his high school class and had earned three letters in football and basketball; and Abraham H. Dohi had won an American Legion essay contest in 1940 on the subject of American democracy.

Park College president William Lindsey Young defended his stand by posing the question, "Is war hysteria making us lose sight of our democratic ideals and the priceless guarantee that all Americans are free, equal, and to have the same opportunities?" The *Star Times* editors agreed with the college president: "The motives of the war would be reduced to hypocrisy if the sensible attitude of Dr. Young does not prevail in this and similar controversies," the editors wrote. "If the United States cannot attain victory without emulating the intolerance of its enemies, it would not deserve the victory once it is won."

Telegrams and letters poured into Park College's mailbox. The overwhelming majority supported Young's stand, but a few sided with the mayor. Lyddia Klamm Zeigler of Fort Dodge, Iowa, and a Park alumna urged the college to keep its student body white. "We had foreigners in my class at Park," she wrote. "They were unhappy and so was I about the situation." And Elton B. Hunt reminded the college administrators, "there is a war," while Claude A. Tyler, a self-designated "100% American," warned, "its [*sic*] all a 'front' with them [the Japanese] so don't be fooled by your 'jap' students there, they are out for our blood." Miss Elzoe Clark declared emphatically: "We have found no matter how much they say they are LOYAL AMERICANS there is still the matter of BLOOD IS THICKER THAN WATER and once a JAP always a JAP. I am for eliminating the Jap families for generations down out of the United States."

On the other side of the divide, the Reverend Charles E. Andrus of Ashland, Kansas, observed: "It seems as though the Mayor of Parkville needs a little Christianity." And Dr. Ruth E. Snyder of New York City added that there should be no question about the admissibility of nisei students "if Park is what it professes to be—a democratic, Christian college." A group of four Park alumni wrote to the college president: "How I wish my boot was long enough to reach the pants and especially the seat of Parkville's mayor and other pseudo patriotic Isolationists. . . . By all means take in as many Japanese students of high quality like the three you have."

"The battle of Park College is ended and seven American-born

Japanese will enroll as students this fall over the protests of the Mayor, the Councilmen and many of the 675 townspeople," the Associated Press reported on September 5, 1942. Despite the mayor's threats, the college's trustees voted to support the president's decision and admit five nisei men and two women in the fall semester. That vote was urged by "a cross-section" of the students at Park College, who signed a petition noting that "it is our patriotic duty to permit a limited number of American-born students of Japanese descent to continue their education in this institution." As if to conclude "the battle of Parkville" a mere six months later, one of those nisei students, Masaye Nagao, wrote: "I'm very happy here at Park. As I have probably written to you before, the spirit of the school and the students is wonderful! True friendships and the Christian spirit are in evidence everywhere. My association with these fine people has given me a brighter outlook for the future."[25]

A common thread, if one exists, in these letters between nisei students and Student Relocation Council staff members is the gratitude of the students for the Council's role in extricating them from the concentration camps and enabling their education and hence their futures. "The relocation of students has affected me greatly," wrote Albert K. Mineta to the Council's Tom Bodine in November 1942, "for after evacuation of the West Coast was announced, I, as well as hundreds of other students, knew not where to apply or to turn for information and guidance. However, thanks to the members of the committee . . . , the nucleus of an organization designed to handle this problem was created in the midst of great uncertainty and confusion. . . . If it had not been for your untiring efforts, I doubt if I would be fortunate enough to attend college this year." Ruth Hide Dohi added: "It was most splendid of you [Tom Bodine] to obtain the travel permit for me; I am very, very grateful to you, indeed, for this and for your many kind letters."[26]

Another aspect of that thread of gratitude was the keen desire of some of the students to please the Council and its staff who tried to instill, especially among the first group of nisei student relocatees, a sense of responsibility to the students who would follow them and, indeed, for the entire program of student relocation. Their academic performance and social interactions, the nisei students were told, would help to determine the fate of this experiment in American democracy. If they should falter academically or somehow elicit hostility from their student peers, instructors, or local communities through their behavior, the argument went, educational institutions and their adjacent communities might not welcome the next group of Japanese American students. That feeling of responsibility and debt incurred through the Council's work on their behalf weighed heavily in the minds of some of the nisei correspondents.

"In one sense, those of us who have been released from the relocation centers are pioneers and are responsible for introducing ourselves and others of Japanese ancestry to the American public in the East," wrote a nisei relocatee. "Our task is to act and think in such a way as to create a favorable public opinion toward Japanese-Americans. As one who is 'out,' I shall do my best to further that end." Another explained, "my job will not only be one of studying hard, but also one of cultivating good public relations with the Caucasians whom I will be coming in contact with, so that I may pave the way for more Japanese-Americans who might be interested in attending school."[27]

Kiyo Sato reflected upon student life at Hillsdale College in Hillsdale, Michigan, in March 1943. "Since coming to Hillsdale, on October 11, I have been getting along very well," Sato reported. "The students and people here are understanding and kind." But Sato's ambition exceeded that of most students, because she represented an entire people and was a model for other nisei students who would follow in her footsteps. "I realize the responsibility I have," Sato wrote. "Most of the people here in Hillsdale have not seen a Japanese face before and also many of them have not heard of evacuation. . . . I don't know how I can ever thank you for this opportunity," Sato acknowledged. "I hope to prove worthy of such a chance."[28]

Yearbook

Portraits

"THE EVENTS OF THE past nine months," wrote Naomi Iwasaki on September 3, 1942, "have completely altered the plans and hopes that I wished to fulfill." She had entered the University of California, Los Angeles, in the fall of 1941 as a business major, and had planned to take over her father's business, a chain of retail produce markets in Los Angeles and vicinity, when he retired. Instead, the war and removal and detention orders changed all that. Iwasaki and her family were confined at Heart Mountain concentration camp in Wyoming, "segregated and shut out from the active outside world," and "we were limited in our opportunity to learn new things and to better ourselves." Her determination to leave the camp and complete her college education thus was strengthened by the realization of education's value and the challenges of a postwar reconstruction. "I am, therefore," Iwasaki stated, "going to attend college with the idea and purpose of preparing myself so that I can be of use and help to others as well as myself, so that I will be an asset to my community and to humanity in the postwar period."[1]

But the nisei were not free simply to "attend college," no matter how determined or prepared. That was the point. They were dependent on others to open the doors that had been shut to them. The University of Kansas City's school of dentistry was long noted among Japanese Americans as one of the few dentistry schools in the country that accepted them. Perhaps its first nisei student was Samuel Otoichi Fujii from Lihue, Kauai, who graduated in 1929. Others followed him, and by World War II, the school had a reputation among Japanese Americans from Hawaii as a place to go. "The boys from Hawaii knew of prior graduates of UMKC [University of Missouri–Kansas City] from the '20s and '30s from Hawaii," explained George Tanaka, a past president of the UMKC Dental Alumni Association. "Naturally they would apply there."[2]

Aspiring nisei dentists had few options for training before World War II, but this was even more of a problem during and immediately after the war. "You have to understand that at the time it was not easy for Japanese-Americans from anywhere, be it Hawaii or California, to get into professional schools during the war or at the tail end of the war," recalled Robert Nagamoto, whose father, George Nagamoto, was an instructor in oral pathology at the University of Kansas City's school of dentistry in 1944 after being released from camp. "There were still strong feelings against them." During this time of particular need, Japanese Americans were aided by the school's dean, Roy J. Rinehart, who took a special interest in the nisei students. "I applied to several dental schools in the east and most of them didn't want to take a chance," Peter Yoshitomi remembered. "Three colleges accepted us [nisei], but most of the boys relocated to the University of Kansas City under Dean Rinehart. We were treated very well, and I appreciate what Dean Rinehart and his staff did for us so that we were able to graduate. I'm grateful for that; he was a wonderful man. As you can understand, those were hard times for us. And I'm grateful that I was able to complete my schooling."[3]

William W. Hall, Jr., the College of Idaho's president, was also instrumental in opening the doors of his institution to nisei students. "December 7, 1941," he recalled, "came just a month after the celebration of the fiftieth anniversary of the college, which was featured by the dedication of two new buildings, a gymnasium and a chemistry hall. That celebration proved to be more than the celebration of an anniversary. It marked the end of an era with respect to the experience and expectations of youth." Innocence and optimism were casualties of the war. Idaho's Japanese Americans, Hall remembered, were mainly truck farmers much admired by the state's residents because of their "industriousness and qualities of good citizenship." News that a nisei student had won a competitive scholarship to the College of Idaho "received favorable publicity and comment in the valley papers. All of this changed during the early afternoon of Sunday, December 7."⁴

Signs prohibiting service to Japanese Americans went up in restaurants, barbershops, pool halls, and even in some churches. The nisei student who had been awarded a scholarship that summer told the college president that she feared riding the buses. There were reports of "direct violence," but these were "discreetly hushed up." A WRA-run concentration camp was built in south central Idaho, and a camp for Japanese American laborers and their families was established on the outskirts of a nearby town.

Because of those centers for Japanese Americans, the College of Idaho received applications from prospective nisei students and a letter from the Presbyterian Board of Christian Education "urging that we assist these luckless youngsters and inquiring whether we were in a position to offer scholarships or other concessions," recalled Hall. "We had several Japanese-American students at the college. More were on their way from the coast. . . . I knew that in pursuing a liberal policy toward Japanese-Americans I could count upon the support of the student body and the faculty and the covert if not overt hostility of most of the townspeople."

Faced with that situation and prospect, the college president presented the matter to his board of trustees. "After a certain amount of mumbling in their beards," remembered Hall, "the members . . . agreed that Japanese-Americans should be treated on the same basis as other American students." The president proceeded to admit all of the qualified nisei applicants who could pay their fees. Thus, Hall wrote, "in the midst of the war while local hostility ran high twenty-one Japanese-Americans out of a reduced civilian enrolment of about two hundred were registered at The College of Idaho. So far as I know, this was the largest number in proportion to the student body of any college in this country. Nobody publicized the fact, nobody gave us any credit for it. . . . It was the most eloquent tribute that could have been paid to the spirit of the place," declared the college president with deserved pride. "Intolerance may invade Main Street but it doesn't get by the gate at The College of Idaho. Everybody sensed this almost instinctively."

Indeed, listed among the first-year students at the College of Idaho in 1942 were Grace Nishioka, George Koyama, and Warren Tamura, who was described as a "hard blocking quarterback" and "a hard tackling line-backer on defense" in that year's annual student publication, *The Trail*. The following year, Grace Kumazawa from Nyssa, Oregon, was pictured among the college's juniors; Grace Nishioka, George Koyama, and Warren Tamura had become sophomores; and among the first-year students were Mary Doi, Isaac and Masako Endow, Kimiko Fujii, Hiram Hachiya, Ken Inaba, Kate and Taka Iwasaki, Fred Kondo, Sachi Munekata, George Nagasaka, Ken Otani, George Saito, Lea and May Uchiyama, Chiyo Yamada, and Ted Yasuda.

Nisei students participated in a number of extracurricular activities. Warren Tamura was joined by George Saito on the college football team, Fred Kondo played guard for the basketball team, and Ken Otani and Fred Kondo were members of the baseball team. Grace Nishioka headed the publicity committee of the Boone Christian Association and was secretary of the International Relations Club, Chiyo Yamada joined the Shield, an honorary service organization, and Grace Kumazawa was a member of the science club, Philotech. In 1944, sophomores Kimiko Fujii and Taka Iwasaki joined the Women's Athletic Association, whose members swam and played hockey, volleyball, basketball, and softball in season, and participated in badminton, archery, tennis, ping-pong, and bicycling.[5]

Many institutions, guided by their trustees and probably by the notion that clusters of Japanese Americans would incur unwanted attention, established quotas on the numbers of nisei students they would admit. The University of Utah, for example, initially accepted nisei students on the same basis as any other student. "We," wrote Utah's president, "shall be just and fair with them [nisei] as we would be with any other American-born people." By May 1943, there were 125 nisei students at the University of Utah, 100 of whom were men and 25, women. The vast majority, 100 of them, were out-of-state residents. During the summer and fall of that year, however, hostility against the nisei brought the matter of their admission before the university's regents. On November 11, 1943, the regents voted unanimously to limit the total number of nisei students at the University of Utah to 150.[6]

A few institutions, nonetheless, like the College of Idaho and University of Nebraska, did not have quotas. Patrick Sano remembered being turned down by institutions that had met their limits on nisei students, but the University of Nebraska accepted his request for admission despite having filled its quota. "Nebraska's personal concern and belief in equality transcended the quota system and wartime restrictions," Sano observed, "considering me not as an enemy, but restoring my rightful place among citizens." "I greatly admired Chancellor [Chauncey S.] Boucher, who opened the school to the Student Relocation Center so that students could finish their education," added Dolas Okawaki Koga, a native of Nebraska who was attending the university when fellow niseis from the concentration camps arrived on campus.

About fifty nisei students were admitted to the University of Nebraska in the fall of 1942. Y. J. Fujimura enrolled at Nebraska when he could find no other Midwest school that would admit him, and Richard Morita remembered being accepted at Bowling Green but the townspeople refused to accept him. He thus attended the University of Nebraska. Patrick Sano recalled his apprehension over leaving Poston concentration camp for Lincoln. "Although friends cautioned me of potential violent retaliation from irate citizens who lost sons, family members or relatives in the Pacific war," said Sano, "I left Poston with the endorsement from my mother who believed in the goodness of people and the providence of God. My mother's optimism and faith proved to be true. Neither hatred nor violence, predicted by my friends, were heard or committed in Nebraska. Instead, the people called Nebraskans manifested amity and brotherhood."

There were, nonetheless, incidences of hostility on the University of Nebraska's campus. Kazuo Kimura remembered his discussion with the dean of pharmacy in 1944. When he asked the dean's advice on graduate schools in the pharmaceutical sciences, Kimura recalled, "Dean Burt looked at me in a hostile manner . . . [and said] 'Why does a Jap boy like you want a Ph.D.?'" And yet the university's open door enabled the nisei to resume control over their lives. "After being refused enrollment by many schools," wrote Nora Maehara Mitsumori, "I was very grateful for being accepted to a major university and appreciated the kindness extended to me by the faculty, students and community—an experience I will never forget. Nebraska restored my faith in people." And K. George Hachiya added, "The good

Nebraska experience helped erase the bad memories of the relocation and direct me toward the future."[7]

Like the College of Idaho and University of Nebraska, Grinnell
College was an early supporter of nisei student relocation and admitted them "on the same basis as any other student," in the words of
its president, Samuel Stevens.[8] The first four nisei students arrived at
the Iowa campus through the efforts of Joseph Conard, a Grinnell
graduate, and his uncle, Henry Conard, who was dean of the faculty.
They included Barbara Takahashi, a graduate of Roosevelt High
School in Los Angeles and ranked first in a class of 531; Akiko Hosoi,
a classmate of Takahashi's and ranked fifth; William Kiyasu, a second-
year transfer student from the University of California, Berkeley, and
an honor student in mathematics; and Hisaji Sakai, from San Francisco. In addition to those students, Alan Yamakawa, a physics
instructor, was hired by the college in the fall of 1942. Taduko
Inadomi, Toshio Uyeda, and Coolidge Wakai enrolled at Grinnell the
following year, and Katsuro Murakami and Jane Kobukata arrived in
September 1944. In all, Grinnell College admitted fifteen nisei students during the war.[9]

Grinnell provided financial aid for those nisei students and found
work for them. Tuition totaled $1,000 per year, and most of the stu-
dents, whose families were wards of the government in concentration camps, depended on scholarships and grants from the National
Student Relocation Council and the college. Scholarship help at Grinnell came from a fund created during the Great Depression through
cuts in faculty and staff salaries. Still, nisei students like Hisaji Sakai
had to call upon their families for assistance. Sakai remembered his
sister's sacrifice: "Indelibly etched on my mind is that day when my
eldest sister withdrew and gave me her life-savings of $700.00 so that
I could have an education that was denied her," recalled Sakai. "It is
because my family is willing to take the financial gamble in the most
uncertain of times, that, I, a high school student, and not another
more deserving, find myself at Grinnell."[10] Sakai eventually withdrew
from the college and transferred to the University of Michigan
because of Grinnell's tuition.

Recalling her years at Grinnell, Barbara Takahashi was grateful for
the college's "generosity of spirit" and its "fantastic" and prompt
response to her application. The yearbook noted that Takahashi was

a member of the YWCA and secretary-treasurer and president of the League of Women Voters, she was invited to join the Crescendo Club, an honorary music organization, was a member of the Women's Honor Group, and was an athlete described as "star volleyball flash." "I almost left after my junior year," Takahashi admitted, "but after Hosoi and Sakai left I didn't think it would be nice since they [the college faculty and administration] were so nice." She graduated in 1946 with an art major. "I had a few rocks thrown at me, but we survived," Takahashi summed up her years at Grinnell. "No, it wasn't the most wonderful experience of my life but it was the time."[11]

Hisaji Sakai shared Takahashi's bittersweet memories of Grinnell conditioned by the times, those years of internment and exile. "The Grinnell experience was incredibly enriching and I am grateful for all those who made it possible—but I am not yet ready to extend it to the government," Sakai wrote in 1984. "There were moments of depression and exasperation because of my family's incarceration, and at times Grinnell would unfairly become the focus of my resentment." But Sakai also experienced a clash of cultures wherein an "unsophisticated fishmonger's son from California" was placed in Grinnell, "pure middle America—white, Anglo-Saxon, protestant, and mostly Republican in attitude," where there were a few Catholics, fewer Jews, and no African Americans. Coats and ties were the standard wear for dinner, recalled Sakai, and he managed to attend dances dressed in his lone suit, when "formal" affairs meant white tie and tails and "semiformal" meant black tie. So despite the "goodness and charity" of Grinnell's students and faculty, reflected Sakai, he felt "almost but not quite, a part of the College family."[12]

Some of their white classmates held recollections at slight variance with those nisei students. "On the whole," remembered Ruth Berglund Ryder, "I think most students . . . considered them [Japanese American students] a part of their student body. Faculty felt likewise." And Georgianna Smith explained, "I suspect that we [white students] went out of our way to treat the Japanese-Americans cordially. I did." She added, "This was an era in which Jews were only barely acceptable on this Iowa campus—and there were far more rumors of this problem than of that showing prejudice against Nisei." Away from the college, however, from the "especially protected environment that keeps me from the real world," in the words of Hisaji

Sakai, some residents of Grinnell, Iowa, might have held a different opinion of the college nisei. Ryder recalled that the "townspeople were a bit hostile towards them [the nisei]—wouldn't allow them in stores, movies (one in town) and would not serve them food on occasion—even when they were with other college students."[13]

Perhaps in response to the fears of parents and prospective students in the concentration camps generated by that sort of reception, four nisei students at Simpson College in another Iowa town, Indianola, wrote an open letter "to our friends in relocation camps" published in the college's 1944 yearbook, the *Zenith*. "In answer to your letter of concern and anxiety," the four students began, "we hope that this letter will assure you that we have become quite attached to the Simpson campus and are very contented here. The local residents, our fellow students, and the instructors have all been just 'swell' to us and have taken a personal interest in our welfare." That welcome and the freedoms of life on the outside contrasted with the "hostile and rugged camp life, which we could hardly consider home," the students pointed out. "You do not know how wonderful it is to be accepted into a community again without any regard to our ancestral background. Here at Simpson College, through our daily associations, we have found everything that is American in spirit."[14]

Those nisei students were not alone in their yearning for the "American spirit." White students at the University of Kansas, in their broadside, *The Gadfly*, scored the hypocrisy of fighting a war for democracy abroad while denying those rights and privileges to racial minorities at home. The November 11, 1943, issue observed that "races regarded as inferior will ultimately rise up in violent conflict with those who forcibly assert their superiority," and cited as evidence the 1943 "race riots" in Detroit, Los Angeles, Harlem, and Beaumont, Texas. It also condemned the exclusion of Japanese American students from the University of Kansas by the board of regents, who had voted in the spring of 1942 to deny admittance to nisei students in the Kansas state schools. Despite several appeals for a reconsideration of their decision by "representative bodies" of the university and adjacent colleges and universities, the regents refused "to touch this controversial question." *The Gadfly*'s editors contended that "the majority of the student body who have ever thought over the question is wondering why Japanese-American students do not attend this university," and

urged students and administrators "to wipe this disgrace to democ-
ractic education from the University of Kansas."[15]

The *Berea Citizen* reported on January 8, 1942, that two students
from Hawaii had enrolled at Berea College. "The newly developed
war has caught two young men a long way from home," the Berea,
Kentucky, paper noted. Richard Wong and Tommy Okuma of Honolulu and students at the University of Hawaii were attending a
national conference of Christian students held at Miami University
in Oxford, Ohio, when the Japanese attack on Pearl Harbor left them
stranded on the mainland. Both decided to attend Berea College, and
received a warm reception. "Both the boys have enrolled in Berea College," the newspaper reported. "Richard is an English student and
Tommy is a psychology major. Both think Berea is a nice place. Tommy
says that 'The sudden hospitality here is more than comparable with
that of Honolulu.'"

Later the following year, on November 18, 1943, the *Citizen*
reported that the local Civilian Defense Council had passed a resolution against the relocation of any Japanese Americans to Berea. The
issue was hotly debated, the report noted, but the final outcome was
based on the fears that relocated Japanese Americans "endangered the
safety of the U.S." and their presence in Berea might cause "grave disturbances." The council's action failed to put the matter to rest, because
individuals and groups continued the debate in the *Citizen*'s letters
section mainly in opposition to the resolution. Mrs. James G. Wash-
burn declared that "no one has any reason to become excited or worried over the loyalty of a group of American citizens of Japanese
blood," and observed that it would be unfortunate if her husband,
who at the time was serving in the military, and others were to learn
"that there are persons in their home town who wish to undermine
the very things for which they are fighting by wishing to deny the
rights of citizenship to loyal Americans." William G. Klein asked
whether the council's resolution violated "the provisions in the Constitution guaranteeing the civil rights of all citizens," or were in accord
with "the life and teachings of our Lord Jesus Christ"?[16]

A veteran of World War I and member of the Civilian Defense
Council explained his vote to exclude Japanese Americans from his
Kentucky town. "It is my opinion," the letter writer identified only
as "J. D." offered, "that you cannot educate a rattlesnake so that his

grandson won't bite you." But Louise Young, president of Berea College's YWCA, countered: "As students we are ready to aid those whose educations have been utterly disrupted, largely through no fault of their own, except that they are of Japanese ancestry. As Christian students we have pledged to 'unite in the desire to realize full and creative life through a growing knowledge of God. We determine to have a part in making this life possible for all people.'" Thus, Young reported, Berea College's YWCA cabinet voted unanimously to urge the administration to allow relocated nisei students to study at the college.[17] Indeed, included in the 1943 Berea College yearbook, the *Chimes,* are Thomas Okuma senior psychology major from Honolulu and Mary Takagaki of Salt Lake City and secretary of the junior class, and in the 1949 *Chimes* are Frank Seto, a senior biology major from San Francisco, and Nobuyuki Yokogawa from Los Angeles and a senior physics major.[18]

Nisei college students, like their white supporters, raised their voices in opposition to injustices. Hattie Masuko Kawahara transferred to Mount Holyoke College in South Hadley, Massachusetts, in the fall of 1943. She had attended Reed College in Portland, Oregon, from September 1939 to June 1942, when the military's removal orders interrupted her education. She aspired to a high school teaching career or work as a librarian, but her first love was, as she put it, researching "post-war problems."[19] Kawahara's essay, "I Am an American," was published in the August 1944 issue of *Mademoiselle* magazine. The article followed a series of discussions sponsored by the magazine for college women on the contemporary problems of democracy.

In her essay, Kawahara explained that the nisei were "products of the American environment and culture," and that "we may look Japanese but in our hearts and thinking we belong to the country of our birth." Dolls and baseball, Superman and Dick Tracy, and ice cream sodas, jazz, and the movies were all intimate parts of the nisei experience. "We know no other life except that which we have had here in America," Kawahara wrote. Thus, Pearl Harbor and the mass removal of Japanese Americans along the West Coast came as "a great blow to our security and hopes," she recalled, "but we never lost faith in the country which is our home." Nisei served in the military, attended colleges, worked on farms, and contributed to the war effort, because, Kawahara stated, "we have a definite stake in the cause for which the war is being fought. The nisei believe in the democratic philosophy which stresses the dignity and the worth of every individual, regardless of color, religion or nationality." Japanese Americans, she continued, knew what it meant to be deprived of those liberties, and as a political science student, "I am acutely aware of the responsibility which rests upon all of us, nisei as well as other Americans, to help create the right kind of world—a world free from discrimination because of color, religion or nationality; a world in which individual liberty is guaranteed by law; and a world in which a certain standard of living and economic security are provided for all." Kawahara offered a global vision, because, she concluded, "the world is one."

Indeed some nisei students connected racism directed against Japanese Americans with racism generally. Kenji Okuda was a transfer student from the University of Washington who arrived at Oberlin College in January 1943. "The reception I received at Oberlin was certainly very positive—incredible, I would say. . . . Perhaps as an indication of widespread student objection to the evacuation, or as a gesture of defiance," recalled Okuda, "I was asked within a few weeks of my arrival to run for president of the student council. To my surprise, I was elected to a one-year term." In 1944, during a Student Christian Movement conference in Wooster, Ohio, Okuda remembered, "I was involved in a series of sit-ins in Wooster restaurants that refused to serve blacks."[20]

Matsuye Taoka recalled a lesson she learned during World War II. "I'm still a little self-conscious in any group outside our friends," she said. "I feel a certain kinship with all minority groups." A graduate of Stanford University, Taoka and her husband, George, tried to find a place to stay in Toledo, Ohio, in 1943. George was a graduate student at the University of Toledo, the only school that accepted him of more than a dozen to which he had applied, and the Taokas had difficulty finding a place to live. "We finally got a place at the Belvedere Apartments, maybe because the caretaker was black," Matsuye remembered. "The owner wanted to evict us when he found out that we were Oriental. We went to his home with the caretaker and talked to him. He finally said that if it was all right with the caretaker, it was all right with him."[21]

Frederick Hayashi was, like Berea College students Richard Wong and Tommy Okuma, from Hawaii and stranded on the mainland because of the war and the Army's imposition of martial law in the islands.[22] In the fall of 1938, when he was nineteen years old and a sophomore in high school, Hayashi had expressed his desire to study the piano at either New England Conservatory or Oberlin College, and in preparation planned to study braille music at the Perkins Institution and Massachusetts School for the Blind. Hayashi was blind from birth, but had sufficient vision to travel by himself. He had, reported the director of Hawaii's agency for the blind, "considerable musical training," and was "quite talented as a pianist," according to a Perkins summary in Hayashi's file.[23] His high school principal in Wahiawa, in recommending him to the Perkins' director, wrote that Hayashi was "an excellent student, always cheerful, cooperative and enthusiastic. I have every good reason to believe that he will make good at Perkins Institution and also in Oberlin if ever he is admitted there."[24]

In the spring of 1939, Hayashi's educational plans took an unexpected turn because of the sudden death of his father. He was determined to attend Perkins to complete his high school diploma, but his ultimate goal of enrolling at Oberlin seemed unreachable. The family's finances wouldn't allow it. Even the Perkins tuition would be "a real hardship on his family," Hayashi's sponsor wrote, but they were willing to sacrifice to pay the sixty dollars per month tuition and hoped that the youth could work on the school's farm during the summer to earn his room and board.[25]

Hayashi left Hawaii in September 1939, and as he made his way to the mainland and the East Coast, his mother, Asao Hayashi, wrote to the Perkins' director. "My son, Frederick Hayashi, is now on his way to The Perkins Institution for the Blind, crossing both Ocean and the Continent," she began. "It is really his first experience to part with his family and travel to such a far place. Assuming his environment and climate must be differ from that of here, I, as the mother, beg your special guidance for him. I have lost my husband on the early part of this spring," she explained. "Meanwhile, a sense of grief is still heavier on my heart, it is rather unbearable to send him to such a unknown far place." Asao Hayashi's motherly love bore both losses and the financial burden of her son's education. Enclosed in her letter was a money order for sixty dollars for the month of September and her pledge, "I will do my best to fulfill my financial obligation."[26]

The registrar at Perkins responded to Hayashi's letter by reporting that Frederick had arrived "safe and sound" and had been assigned a room at Bridgman Cottage. "I am sure that he will be happy there and in his school work also," the registrar assured. "School has begun this morning with nearly all the pupils present and with bright sunshine and mild temperature." And thinking about Asao Hayashi's concern over New England's weather, the registrar thoughtfully added, "I hope for the sake of those from warm countries that we shall not have a severe winter or, at least, that they will become accustomed to cold weather before it comes."[27]

Frederick Hayashi's progress was reported by the Perkins staff. Hayashi "wishes to take tuning and a great deal of music," a September 1939 report noted, "and also to prepare for college though it is not definite whether or not he will be able to go. . . . Is ambitious and a hard worker." And in January 1940, Hayashi's principal told his mother that Frederick had "considerable difficulty with the English language," but that he had "real talent in music. He works hard, has had some difficulty with the music braille, but is making satisfactory progress. . . . Frederick is a very pleasant boy with whom to work and we are all enjoying him."[28]

Hayashi received his high school diploma at Perkins in June 1942, but the war and the military authorities in Hawaii refused to allow his return to the islands. Following his graduation, he remained at Perkins for a year and enrolled at the Moody Bible Institute in Chicago in June 1943. Hayashi attended classes at the Bible Institute, but also traveled to play for several churches in the vicinity and accompanied a preacher that summer to help with his services in Indiana. A Perkins summary of Hayashi's mainland career probably explained well his situation and problem. "Frederick realized," the report observed, "that he would not be successful in obtaining a job because of the feeling against Japanese but he would like to have had work and to have been self-supporting."[29] Instead, he had to rely on the goodwill of others and the financial support of his mother. Hayashi was finally able to return home to Hawaii in November 1945.

Despite the best of intentions of colleges and universities, government bureaucracy—usually instigated by the military—sometimes stood in the way of nisei education during the war. The University of Minnesota is instructive in that regard, and its circumstance exemplifies the sometimes absurd consequences of the "military necessity" justification for the mass removal and detention of the West Coast Japanese Americans. Historians now know that "military necessity," the ostensible reason for the eviction and confinement orders, from President Roosevelt's Executive Order 9066 to the government's defense of its policies before the U.S. Supreme Court, was false and simply conjured up by the president and executive branch to justify its otherwise unconstitutional actions.[30] As Assistant Secretary of War McCloy said on February 11, 1942, when conveying the president's instructions to the military on the West Coast in anticipation of Executive Order 9066, "do anything you think necessary . . . if it involves citizens, we will take care of them too . . . but it has got to be dictated by military necessity."[31]

Once enunciated, the "military necessity" doctrine was assumed and applied by government bureaucrats in controlling the movements and lives of Japanese Americans. On September 30, 1942, W. C. Coffey, president of the University of Minnesota, Minneapolis, wrote to Secretary of War Stimson, asking about the government's position on nisei students. "The University of Minnesota has been much concerned with the question of the admission of Japanese-American students who have moved from the west coast areas," Coffey began. "We have much hoped that there would be some definite policy formulated by a responsible federal agency that would serve to guide the educational institutions with respect to the acceptance of these students."[32] Coffey's letter was sent to McCloy for his department's response, but he turned the matter over to the War Relocation Authority and National Student Relocation Council who had authority over the student relocation program. The WRA informed Coffey that the University of Minnesota had not yet been cleared to accept nisei students from the concentration camps, but that those who had escaped internment's sweep should be admitted as "any other students of American citizenship." The Navy, however, the WRA response cautioned, objected to the university's acceptance of nisei students from the camps, because Minnesota carried on "confidential training and research for the Navy Department." Indeed, James Forrestal, Navy undersecretary, affirmed that Minnesota was one of the fifty-three colleges and universities and twenty-four vocational schools on the prohibited list for nisei, because they "might reveal information of the activity [Navy research and personnel training] to the enemy or enemy agents." That caution was necessary, Forrestal explained, "to insure security of our war effort."[33]

"I think we are back just where we started!" exclaimed Malcolm M. Willey, university dean and assistant to the president, when commenting on Forrestal's ruling.[34] The university, it had seemed from the WRA communication, was free to accept nisei students who were not from the camps, but the Navy's interdiction barred them from the campus completely. So the university initiated a series of memoranda with the WRA and National Student Relocation Council to explain to them Minnesota's predicament regarding Japanese American students. The university could not accept nisei students under orders from the Navy, Willey wrote, and the WRA and Council expressed their disappointment with Minnesota for not accepting those students at its farm campus away from the Navy research work at the main campus. The two campuses were not separated, Willey replied, and the Navy had a training school on the farm campus.[35]

At the end of the 1942–43 academic year, Minnesota's Coffey wrote to Forrestal inquiring if there had been any changes in the Navy's ruling for his campus. "The University of Minnesota still receives applications from Japanese-American students who wish to enter here and there are many in our local community who do not understand why we have refused to admit them, especially since some other institutions in the immediate vicinity have done so," the president explained. Forrestal informed Coffey that instead of a contraction of prohibitions, the list of excluded institutions had grown to ninety-three. The situation still warranted that policy, he wrote, "to prevent information of value to the enemy from falling into possession of those who are or may be inimical to the interests of the United States." And, he added, "I am sure you also recognize the importance of this problem and that while our nation is fighting for the maintenance and preservation of principles and doctrine that have made it great, any doubts arising must be resolved in favor of the United States, regardless of apparent injustice and hardship."[36]

Perhaps recognizing the contradictions in the Navy's position, Coffey wrote a brief note to his assistant, Willey, that this latest policy statement "really makes our situation relative to the admittance of Japanese-American students worse rather than better." The president had in mind the presence on Minnesota's campus of Japanese American language instructors for training that had been requested by the Army. There were also Japanese Americans who had been cleared by the FBI for leave from the concentration camps, and who were valuable to the university as research scientists and employees. If those posed security risks, why had the FBI released them from detention? Willey, in turn, explained the confused situation to the Army and asked for a resolution. "We have a considerable file bearing on the question in which we have attempted to ascertain what our appropriate policy should be," an exasperated Willey wrote. Five nisei instructors taught Japanese at Minnesota "without causing the slightest difficulty," he observed, yet nisei students and Japanese American employees were barred from campus by Navy order.[37]

The Army replied that the security provisions were still in force, but that Japanese Americans, both students and university employees, could now be admitted and hired on a case-by-case basis. On November 20, 1943, Minnesota's regents approved the policy of admitting nisei students and employing Japanese Americans subject to military clearance.[38] Thus from the fall of 1943 to the fall of 1944, when the restrictions were finally lifted, the University of Minnesota had to request and obtain clearance from the military for each of its nisei students and staff members. In addition, the university had to comply with specific conditions upon which depended the individual's presence at Minnesota. A nisei language instructor, for example, was allowed on Minnesota's campus by the Army only on the condition that the person be "placed under surveillance" and "not be allowed access to classified information, documents and similar matters." "If the above mentioned conditions are not acceptable," ruled the Army, "it will be necessary to terminate . . . [the instructor's] employment and this office should be so advised."[39] In those ways, higher education was recruited as an accomplice, both willing and otherwise, in the government's interventions in the lives and freedom of its citizens.

The "military necessity" rationale provided sufficient reason for the exclusion of the nisei from several institutions. When Robert G. Sproul, president of the University of California, Berkeley, asked institutions east of the Sierra Nevada to accept nisei students in the spring of 1942, the Utah State Agricultural College trustees replied that the

Logan campus would be closed to Japanese Americans because "the school is crowded with a naval training program, giving elementary and advanced classes in radio technology to a large number of naval trainees." And the Alumni Association of the University of Nevada and the state's Bar Association wrote letters to the university's board of regents opposing the admission of nisei students. It might appear paradoxical, the Alumni Association's president wrote, to deny educational freedoms to Americans while fighting a war to preserve democracy, but "we cannot but feel that Japanese have forfeited all right to such consideration. . . . Is there any guarantee that present or contemplated Japanese students will not continue the work of espionage?" Further, the association's president argued, the Japanese were being removed from the coastal areas because they constituted a military menace. "Their presence, it is claimed, is dangerous. Would the danger be any less in their presence in Reno, less than 250 miles from the coast, and in an area included in the western defense command?" Finally, why should "members of a treacherous race" take the seats of men whose education was interrupted by the war and who served in the armed forces and in defense industries?[40]

The University of Nevada's board of regents passed unanimously on May 9, 1942, the policy "that no further matriculations be permitted of persons of Japanese birth or ancestry unless born in the state of Nevada." Indeed, on October 2, 1943, the board was informed that a Japanese American student had been denied admission into the university's mining engineering program, although Tomomi Ito enrolled at the university in January 1943 because he had been born in Fallon, Nevada. And at least three other nisei students attended the university during this period of exclusion because they had been admitted before the regents' prohibition. On September 22, 1945, the regents voted unanimously to rescind the exclusion policy.[41]

Flipping through the pages of college yearbooks, portraits emerge of nisei students that defy simple classification. They are as various, as distinctive as the campuses to which they went. Agnes Yamamoto, whose parents were interned in Amache, Colorado, graduated from Saint Mary's College in Indiana in 1946 with a bachelor's degree in social science. While a student, Yamamoto was a member of the International Relations Club, the Thomists, and the Women's Athletic

Association. She translated poetry from the Japanese for *Chimes,* a student literary journal, was on the college honor roll, headed the program committee for the annual sports day in 1944, and worked on the staff of the college yearbook, the *Blue Mantle.*[42]

Albert Nakazawa, who attended Valparaiso University in the fall of 1942, was a Methodist in a predominantly Lutheran school. Nakazawa became a member of the largest of six campus fraternities, and played in the backfield of the university's 1942 football team. The student newspaper mentioned Nakazawa in one issue, reporting him as the "speedster, [who] carried the ball to the 12-yard line for a first down."[43]

Andy Hasegawa, Mitsuo Yamada, and Tom Haritani played on Baker University's basketball team in Baldwin City, Kansas, and were described by the 1944 Baker yearbook as, "three Japanese-American students, who turned in top performances all year. . . ." And Hannah Tani and Kate Kyono served as secretary and vice president, respectively, of the Independent Organization, a member of the National Independent Student Association and a sponsor of various programs and activities on campus.[44]

The 1945 graduating class at Washington University in St. Louis, Missouri, included Ralph Akamine from Hilo, Hawaii; Masaki Nakauchi from Hanford, California; Masashi Yamada, who was the manager of the basketball team and Cosmopolitan Club member; and architectural students Gyo Obata and George Matsumoto. Obata served as president of the Architectural Society during the 1944–45 school year, a member of the student senate, and art editor for the *Hatchet.* George Shimizu, another member of the 1945 class, was "the number two hurler" on the baseball team and compiled a three-and-three record that season.[45]

A transfer student from Linfield College, Oregon in 1942, Mitsue Endow enrolled at William Jewell College in Liberty, Missouri. On her application, Endow declared her religious preference as "Quaker," and her life's work as "pyscho-sociological." During her three years at William Jewell, Endow was a member of the Young Women's Auxiliary, a Christian service organization, Theta Chi Delta, a national honorary chemistry society, Zeta Kappa Epsilon, an honorary history society, the Northern-Eastern States Club comprised of students from north of the Mason-Dixon line, the Women's Athletic Association, the Independent Society, the Glee Club, Chess Club, and International Relations Club. She served on the staff of the *Tatler,* and was elected secretary-treasurer of Theta Chi Delta and the Northern-Eastern States Club, treasurer of the Women's Athletic Association, made the fall 1945 honor roll with the highest mark, and as a senior was selected to the Phi Epsilon Honor Society on the basis of scholarship and service.[46]

Ben Iijima attended Drew University in Madison, New Jersey. "How familiar a sight it was to see Ben, hands in pockets, hurrying across campus to the dining hall, his face glowing with that friendly smile!" wrote the editors of Drew's 1944 yearbook. "Whether on the basketball court or in a bull session, Ben enjoyed the company of his fellow students. He was one of those rare individuals who finds great joy in simply listening to and watching others." Described as "full of life," Iijima was the secretary-treasurer of his class, baseball manager, and member of the debate squad, international relations club, and student life and welfare committee. Also at Drew was John Kikuchi, nicknamed "Jackson" and described as "dapper" by the 1944 yearbook editors. "Always dressed in the latest style, he presented an impeccable appearance," the editors wrote of "Jackson." "With his pants pegged according to the newest fashion, a 'sharp' sports jacket, and the latest tune on his lips, he was always ready for a quick jaunt to the skating rink or a weekend excursion to New York." This "bon vivant," however, had a "serious side," majoring in biochemistry and taking "a stiff schedule" of courses.[47]

Sisters, Sato-ko and Chiyo-ko Oguri, attended Barnard College in New York City. The 1943 yearbook, *Mortarboard,* described the elder Sato-ko as "friendly, sincere, an understanding and delightful companion . . . loves music, ballet, theatre, and her major zoology." Sato-ko, the editors wrote, was "sweet and charming" and planned to pursue a position as a laboratory technician. Chiyo-ko was a chemistry major who, like Sato-ko, loved zoology. Indeed, Chiyo-ko, the 1944 *Mortarboard* editors wrote, was "an animal lover whose affections are large enough to include the feline species. . . . [And she was also] fond of the ballet."[48]

Students from Hawaii at Kansas State University, Manhattan, Kansas, included Vernon K. Sato, a first-year mechanical engineering student in 1942 from Kalaheo, Kauai, a member of the Cosmopolitan Club (organized to promote international understanding on campus), a member of the American Society of Mechanical Engineers and 4-H Club, and a weight lifter, member of the freshman swim team, and a participant in intramural softball and basketball; Roy Nagakura, a first-year agricultural student in 1942 from Hilo, and a member of the ROTC and Cosmopolitan Club; Howard Furumoto, a first-year agriculture student in 1942 from Ninole, Hawaii, a member of the ROTC and president of the Cosmopolitan Club, a member of the Hawaiian Club, YMCA, and Alpha Zeta (an honorary society selected from the top two-fifths of a class on the basis of character and leadership); and Harvey Harakawa, a sophomore mechanical engineering student in 1942 from Honolulu, a member of the ROTC, YMCA, and the American Society of Mechanical Engineers, an officer of the Cosmopolitan Club, and the recipient of a letter in swimming.[49]

Attending Ashbury College in Wilmore, Kentucky, in 1944 were Victor Fujiu and John M. Miyabe. Fujiu was a transfer student from Pacific College in Los Angeles whose family was held at the Amache concentration camp in Colorado. He majored in philosophy and religion, and was described by the yearbook's editors as "a good leader, with technique and new ideas a plenty; he has talents galore, choice wit, and a temperament spry and canty." Miyabe's family was confined at the Poston, Arizona camp, and like Fujiu, had transferred from Pacific College. "Johnny," the yearbook editors wrote, was "the true embodiment of vim, vigor, and vitality; he is outstanding in school work, athletics, and also spirituality."[50]

Tomiko Inouye was born in Independence, Oregon, in 1923, and entered the Oregon College of Education in September 1941, but had to leave when the Army ordered the mass removal in June 1942. In her application to Hillsdale College in Michigan the next year, Inouye offered her reasons for wanting to complete her college education. "Although my parents both spent their youth in Japan, they have always been great promoters of education and American ideals," she began. "They are (and needless to say, I am too) eager for me to continue with my college training if it is at all possible." Hillsdale, Inouye noted, was her choice "for both cultural and vocational reasons. While training for a vocation is essential, I believe it is equally as important to broaden one's intellectual and general academic development to enjoy life to its fullest." Inouye was admitted to Hillsdale in the fall of 1943, and the next year was elected the recording secretary of the Athenians, a social and civic society.[51]

Also at Hillsdale was Kiyo Sato, a Californian whose education at Sacramento Junior College was interrupted by the mass detention. Her life's work, Sato wrote in her application form, was to be a writer or educator, because, she explained, "I believe that education of every individual is most important in the building of a country." Sato entered Hillsdale in the fall of 1942, and she graduated with a psychology degree in 1944. During her two years at Hillsdale, she was a member of the Athenians, biology club, and the *Collegian,* the college newspaper. She was elected to the scholastic honor society, Epsilon Delta Alpha, the highest distinction conferred upon students at Hillsdale.

Yasunori Bright Onoda was born in Cosmopolis, Washington, in 1921, the oldest of four children of an immigrant sawmill laborer and his wife. His first day at Broadway High School in Seattle, wrote Onoda in his Hillsdale College application, was the most memorable of his young educational career. "I can still remember how lonely, helpless, and awed I felt that day as I walked down the corridors half-scared and tired," he recalled. "Maybe this was because I had just enrolled from a small country school. However four years later, June, 1939, I graduated from this school with a Gold Seal Pin." After high school, Onoda worked as an apprentice machinist at the Puget Sound Navy Yard, but in April 1942 was removed with his family to a concentration camp in Idaho. At Hillsdale, Onoda majored in chemistry, and was a member of the biology club, the Independent Men's Organization, and the 1944 football and basketball teams. Like Kiyo Sato, Onoda was inducted into the honorary scholastic society Epsilon Delta Alpha.

The first few months of Thomas T. Sugihara's life in Michigan at Kalamazoo College were "the loneliest that I can remember," he wrote. Sugihara had been a mathematics and science student at Long Beach Junior College in southern California when the mass removal orders changed his life. For several months, he and his parents were confined at Santa Anita Assembly Center. "One of the first things we enterprising students did was to try to figure out how to get out (legally)," Sugihara remembered. His sister worked for the American Baptist Home Mission Society, and she arranged, through the Society, the placement of her brother at Kalamazoo. "I knew nothing of Kalamazoo when I learned that I was going there," confessed Sugihara. But, "I did not hesitate; anything would be better than an internment camp." He arrived in Kalamazoo in October 1942.

Although he was the first of four Japanese American students at Kalamazoo during the war, Sugihara was aided by white friends who, "with a sensitivity unusual at any time, . . . sort of adopted me and gently steered me in the right directions in social and cultural matters. . . . They made every effort to understand how to fit a kid from a blue-collar Asian family into the gracious living epitomized by dinners in Welles Hall," Sugihara recalled gratefully. Social tolerance extended to interracial dating, Sugihara noted. White students "seemed not surprised that I would want female companionship to attend dances or go to movies or coeducational events," he remembered. However, a member of the college staff advised Sugihara's friend that she was "jeopardizing her future" if she continued her relationship with him; and, added Sugihara, "I am certain that the parents of women I dated at Kalamazoo disapproved of our dating at some level or another," including his own mother.

The "capstone" of his college career, Sugihara recalled, was his membership in Kalamazoo's 1944 varsity basketball team. Although the team won only "a few" games, their coach had a picture taken of the team and declared it "the shortest basketball team in the nation." The tallest member was "big" Gus Birtsas at five feet, eleven inches, and the shortest, Tom Sugihara at five feet, four inches. Overall, the team averaged a mere five feet, eight inches. The photograph was a public relations coup for the college, and it appeared in more than 125 newspapers throughout the country, including Panama and Hawaii. The nation's shortest team played against Michigan State, and was dealt "the worst loss a Hornet team ever suffered," Sugihara declared with chagrin and some pride.[52]

The significant numbers of nisei who participated in varsity intercollegiate sports might have been the result of the war, insofar as men and women athletes were drawn away from the college ranks by the armed forces. Hawaii-born Keo Nakama was perhaps an exception. At Ohio State University, Nakama, holder of several freestyle records, and Bill Smith, holder of eight world records, were members of "the greatest swimming team in history." The team took the national title in 1943, and Nakama was chosen team captain of the 1944 and 1945

Buckeye swim teams. Nakama was also a standout baseball player for Ohio State.[53]

Emiko Ishiguro, born and reared in Pennsylvania, entered Wellesley College in the fall of 1941. On the day after Japan's attack on Pearl Harbor, her first-year classmates elected Ishiguro class treasurer. Interviewed in 1990, she recalled that her fellow students and the college administration "never made it an issue that I was Japanese. . . . Wellesley has a very egalitarian spirit. You are here at Wellesley for the individual that you are." But that first Christmas break, concerned with her safety, college officials advised her that it would be unsafe to return home to Pennsylvania by train; so she and her older sister, Mariko, who was a Wellesley senior, remained in the college dormitory. Classmates and faculty invited them to meals, Ishiguro recalled, and gave them Christmas cookies to buoy their spirits. During her years at Wellesley, she participated in crew and fencing, sang in the choir, and headed a dance group. She was a class officer during her first and final years, and was student government treasurer during her junior year. She worked with sailors and patients in army hospitals and with youth in Boston's settlement houses. "Wellesley," Ishiguro stated, "has always been a support for me."[54]

Yearbooks could never reveal the full story of nisei student life. They presented partial and often idealized portraits. The *Wesleyan,* the student newspaper at Nebraska Wesleyan University in Lincoln, announced in its October 23, 1942, issue, "NWU to take Jap students," and by February 1943, Nebraska Wesleyan had admitted seventeen nisei students. Of the university's twenty-six Japanese American students during the war, the careers of Kazuo Tada and Satsuki Hachiya exemplified the successes of the nisei student as chronicled in the *Plainsman,* the school's yearbook.[55]

Tada, from Minidoka concentration camp in Idaho, had transferred to Nebraska Wesleyan from the University of Washington in February 1943. When he graduated in 1946, he had served on the staffs of both the *Wesleyan* and *Plainsman,* played on the university's basketball team as a "hardworking forward," was elected to Phi Kappa Phi, a national honor society chosen from the upper ten percent of the senior class, and was named the "Ideal Plainsman" for 1946 on the basis of "character, scholarship, and personality" as the student who had contributed the most to the university in leadership, activities, and service.

Hachiya entered Nebraska Wesleyan in the fall of 1943 after graduating from the high school at Heart Mountain concentration camp. She was elected to Pi Gamma Mu, a social science honors society, and Psi Chi, an honorary psychology group, served on the student senate, won membership to the Purple Argus, a select honors group of university women students, and like Tada was a member of Phi Kappa Phi. Both Hachiya and Tada graduated in 1946 — Hachiya with a degree in sociology and Tada, in English.

Nisei students like Hachiya and Tada brought distinction to themselves and Japanese Americans broadly, in the minds of many on Nebraska Wesleyan's campus, and they surely had an impact beyond the classroom and basketball court. They introduced to their fellow "Wesleyanites" aspects of their cultures and pasts. Kenji Kurita, from Tule Lake concentration camp in California and a transfer from Oregon's Willamette University in 1943, gave a public lecture about growing up in Hawaii. "I lived on a sugar plantation and walked around barefoot[ed] until I came to college," Kurita remarked and added, "I had never worn an overcoat until I came to Nebraska." Nisei students organized an "Aloha Hop" where a large crowd of colorfully dressed Nebraska Wesleyan students enjoyed a night of "dancing, entertainment and fun, all infused with a real Hawaiian spirit. . . ." On another night at the Co-op, nisei students prepared a sukiyaki dinner followed by a program.

Set against those accomplishments was the sobering record of overall student success at Nebraska Wesleyan as measured by the degree-completion rates of that institution's twenty-six wartime nisei students. Of that total, only ten received their undergraduate degrees from Wesleyan. The remainder transferred to other schools, enlisted in the military, or dropped out. Many were the circumstances of that record, like James Hara who left Nebraska Wesleyan in 1943 to assume a research assistantship at the University of Illinois, Chicago, and Mary Nishi who won a scholarship at the University of California, Los Angeles, after the war's end in 1946. And it is difficult to speculate if Wesleyan's graduation rate mirrors the particularities of that institution or posits a pattern of nisei student mobility during the war. Still, it offers a cautionary note to an otherwise singular and cropped view of nisei education provided by yearbook snapshots.

In the 1945 yearbook of Huron College in Sioux Falls, South

Dakota, four nisei students, Grace Mano, Sei Adachi, Eugene Kodani, and George Hirose, published "an open letter" addressed to the administrators, faculty, and students of the college. Mano was described as "a sociable and ambitious student"; Adachi was an honor student and played guard on the college basketball team; Kodani was a pre-engineering student from Monterey, California; and Hirose had transferred from San Francisco State College. "As the year draws to a close," the students wrote, "we wish to express our sincere appreciation to you for this opportunity we have had to continue our education at Huron College. From our associations with you in just these past several months, we have acquired many sincere friendships, a more intimate understanding of Christianity, and a deepened faith in our America. We came to Huron as perfect strangers from three War Relocation Centers. . . . The majority of you had never known an American of Japanese ancestry before. You were fair and friendly and lived up to our ideals of the American way."[56]

FIVE

A

Thousand

Cranes

JOHN W. NASON, chairman of the National Japanese American Student Relocation Council, reported to the presidents of colleges, universities, and professional schools on November 26, 1942. "We were able to place approximately 330 students in 93 colleges and universities for the first term—in spite of difficulties and obstructions which were not cleared away until the first of August," he submitted of the Council's efforts to date. "The reports which come to us from the colleges and universities which have already received Japanese American students tell a happy story of easy and successful adjustment. The response of many institutions to the challenge of the Japanese American situation is an episode in the history of higher education in this country, of which we may all be proud."[1]

The "Japanese American situation," in truth, was more complicated and mixed than Nason's public relations letter might suggest. Like yearbook portraits, archival documents hide as much as they reveal. All of them must be read with knowing eyes. And they should be supplemented by other sources, like the oral histories and recollections of the nisei students themselves, to add flesh and feeling to the stories preserved on paper. At the same time, reminiscences are fragile documents indeed, subject to the wear of memory and time and to the deliberate craftings of the oral historian and informant. Often the good and the bad stand out in sharper relief when viewed from hindsight, and the everyday routines of study, work, and play grow dim. The total record, in sum, of archival materials, yearbook portraits, and oral history tapes affords the clearest and fullest glimpses of nisei student life during the war.

Masako Amemiya MacFarlane recalled her first reaction to hearing of her acceptance. "Cornell College? No, not the university in New York state. . . . It's in Iowa. Iowa? Yes. Oh. I had no idea where it was nor anything about it, but when told that Cornell College was willing to accept me, I jumped at the opportunity without hesitation. It was an opportunity to leave behind the barbed wire fences, the armed guards, the cramped living quarters, and the line-up with plate and cup in hand for the mess hall." She left her mother, father, sister, and brother for Mount Vernon, Iowa. "The moment I stepped off the train I was warmly greeted by Dean MacGregor and a student, Jan Appelt," MacFarlane remembered. "I felt welcomed and began to feel that I belonged." There were three other nisei students at Cornell College, Yoko Tada, Hank Fujii, and Tom Tashiro; and her two years there were "stimulating, eye-opening, heart-warming years." Students invited her to their homes during the holidays and vacations, and her sister and brother were able to attend her graduation in 1944.[2]

MacFarlane was born in San Francisco in 1920, and grew up in the city's Fillmore district.[3] Her father, Takeshige Amemiya, arrived in San Francisco shortly after the great 1906 earthquake, worked for a time in farm labor, went to Japan to marry Maki Muramatsu, and returned around 1913. Her older sister, Tane, was born in 1917 and younger brother, Minoru, in 1922. MacFarlane held fond memories of growing up in the Fillmore with other nisei children. The family's social life revolved around the First Reform Church and its members. Her mother had grown up in a Christian family and attended Christian mission schools in Tokyo. MacFarlane graduated from Lowell High School, and for a year worked as a maid, the only kind of job that was open to her, she recalled. In the fall of 1939, she entered the University of California, Berkeley, where she was "on the outs" with the nisei crowd, although she joined the Japanese Women's Student Club. Perhaps because of her loneliness, MacFarlane longed to go to a boarding school to get away from the Berkeley scene. But the war intervened, and she and her family were sent to Tanforan Assembly Center.

There MacFarlane learned from the Student Relocation Council about the possibility of attending a college east of the military exclusion zone. She applied, eager to leave the camp. MacFarlane was accepted by Elmhurst College in Illinois and gained her release from Tanforan, but just before she boarded the train, she learned that the local community in Illinois objected to having Japanese Americans in their town, and so her trip was canceled. With nowhere to go, she had to return to Tanforan to await another offer. The Relocation Council promised to find another college for her, and within two days they told her about Cornell College.

The journey, recalled MacFarlane, was the "scarriest train trip I've ever taken." She was greatly excited about leaving until she got on the train. Once on board, she felt uncomfortable, because her fellow passengers eyed her suspiciously and, she surmised, must have wondered about this unaccompanied Japanese American young woman who sat stiffly in her seat. Besides, she noted impishly, she had packed in her bag an alarm clock that ticked loudly. The people around her looked nervous, she thought, eyeing her luggage with its ticking contents. She didn't say a word, and didn't budge from her seat. A kindly African American porter noticed her discomfort and brought her ice cream from the dining car. That helped to relieve some of her tension.

But once in Mount Vernon, Iowa, MacFarlane's "most wonderful reception" made her feel instantly at home. Memorable during her two years at Cornell College were a history professor who invited her to have lunch with him and his wife on their farm outside of town, and her sociology professor who shared with her and other students the joy of bird-watching in the early morning hours. She remembered especially a Christmas spent with a classmate and her family in Des Moines. "They accepted me," she said, and were "just wonderful." She formed a lifetime friendship and correspondence with that student and her family as a consequence. All of the college's students, with the exception of the four nisei, were from the Midwest, MacFarlane observed, and the students, who were mostly women, totaled only about 600, with 78 in her graduating class. Cornell College, she gratefully recalled, gave her the "most wonderful, horizon widening experience I ever had."

Albert Mineta, according to the 1944 yearbook of Drew University in Madison, New Jersey, "was known in the dining hall for the efficient manner in which he performed his headwaiter's duties, in the chemistry lab for the long hours he spent setting up experiments, and in Student Council meetings for his simplified reports on the state of the Student Association Treasury." The yearbook editions noted: "We all knew Al as the quiet and efficient transfer student from the west coast, a boy liked by all for his friendly and gracious manner."[4]

That "quiet and efficient transfer student" was born in San Jose, California, in 1923.[5] His father, Kunisaku, had arrived in Seattle in 1907, and worked his way through various labor camps in the Pacific Northwest down to northern California. He settled in Salinas, married the sister of a friend in Japan, Kane Watanabe, who arrived in San Francisco in 1912 as a "picture bride." The couple farmed vegetables in Salinas, moved to Edenvale in the Santa Clara valley and lived there until about 1920, when they left farming to settle in San Jose's Japantown. There, Kunisaku became an insurance agent, and there, the children, Aya, Etsu, Helen, Albert, and Norman grew up and attended school. After graduating from San Jose High School, Albert entered San Jose State College, but the war broke out and the family was removed in May 1942 to Santa Anita Assembly Center and from there to Heart Mountain concentration camp.

While at Santa Anita, Albert bumped into his former Sunday school teacher, Lester Suzuki. He told Suzuki how much he wanted to continue his college education, but had no money because of the wartime detentions. Suzuki, who was a Methodist minister and had studied at Drew University, a Methodist school, advised Mineta to apply to Drew. He did and one month after having arrived at Heart Mountain, he received a letter from Drew, offering him a tuition scholarship of $400 per year. That amount appears small in retrospect, he said, but at the time it was a "big thing." Indeed, the scholarship enabled him to leave the concentration camp for Drew's campus.

Before Mineta boarded the bus to Billings, Montana, where he planned to catch the train for the East Coast, his mother explained that they could not help him with his education financially because they had no income to speak of in the camp, but she handed him a bankbook showing $1,000 in savings. She had assiduously saved his earnings as a paper delivery boy in San Jose. When he arrived in Madison, New Jersey, Drew's dean greeted him, and Mineta confided that he did not have sufficient funds to pay for his room and board, except for the $1,000. The dean, Mineta remembered, was kind and "very nice," and told him that he could work in the dining room as a waiter for $35 a month and as a chemistry laboratory assistant to cover his room and board. For "fun money," Mineta worked once a week as a babysitter. The earnings from that job he used for square dancing, which he loved, and occasional visits to New York City, where he took in broadway shows.

Student life was filled, Mineta recalled, with a constant round of work and study. The efficient headwaiter and busy chemistry laboratory assistant of Drew's yearbook worked three meals each day in the dining hall and had only every other weekend free for some recreation. The wartime exigencies required that extraordinary effort. Mineta's achievement was gained through his own determined effort and abilities, his parents' emotional support and encouragement, and the assistance of many generous people along the way. He remembered a chemistry professor at San Jose State College who gave him a medical dictionary before he left for the detention camps. She knew of his desire to study medicine, and thought the dictionary would help him retain his interest in the subject. She was right. And many others like her enabled Mineta to graduate from Drew in 1994. The yearbook editors reported: "Al looks forward with anticipation to his future in the field of medicine . . . [and] his years of medical school promise to be successful. Al has the spirit and determination to make them thus."

Besides the racist fences of the wartime concentration camps, nisei women faced the barrier of sexism. Louise Seki Hoare was born in Seattle in 1922.[6] Her mother, Kazu Kuriyama, was highly educated for a woman in Meiji Japan and was a schoolteacher. Her father, Chisato Seki, had migrated to America around 1914. After working for a few years, he returned to Japan, married Kuriyama, and settled in Seattle, where he worked as a salesman. Her mother was sickly and remained at home, recalled Hoare, especially after her two children were born. Because of her mother's frail health, she had to help with the household chores and caring for her younger brother. She felt that her mother must have been lonely and frustrated because of her physical condition, but also because she was unable to make full use of her education and talents. When the family moved to Auburn, a farming community, Hoare continued, her mother's ambition probably dissolved in the mundane routine of farm life and because the women she associated with failed to share her intellectual and cultural interests. Perhaps she took vicarious pleasure in seeing her daughter develop and show promise of fulfilling some of her own aspirations and dreams that could never be.

Hoare attended Auburn's mainly white schools, along with a few other nisei and even fewer American Indians. Japanese American students, noted Hoare, were always placed in the lowest class levels on the assumption that they were not fluent in English and lacked intellectual abilities. But Hoare rose quickly in class standing, despite an unfriendly teacher and despite classmates who made her ashamed of her Japanese lunches and her family's poverty. After graduating from high school, Hoare went on to the University of Washington, but had to return home before the end of the year to care for her ailing mother. Her father had died earlier in the year, and eight months later her mother passed away. Hoare recalled having her mother's ashes sent back to Japan on the last ship that left Seattle before the war. The ship, Hoare said, was the same one that her mother had taken several years earlier to visit her parents.

Hoare returned to the University of Washington after her mother's death, but the war and the mass removal orders threatened to end her education. The Quakers, she said, helped her to board a train and move east of the military zone, and they directed her to Minneapolis. She left Minneapolis and went to Chicago, where she met a woman faculty member on sabbatical leave from Simmons College, in a women's college in Boston. The woman encouraged her to apply to Simmons, and in the fall of 1942, Hoare was enrolled there. Boston and Simmons, Hoare remembered, were "very different from what I was used to," having grown up in the Pacific Northwest. She observed the distinctive ethnic and religious groups and classes that divided Whites and created social hierarchies, and came to understand Boston's neighborhoods that were defined by ethnicity and class.

Hoare received some financial aid through the Student Relocation Council, but mainly depended on the insurance money left by her parents and her part-time work. She majored in biology, despite the prejudice against women in the sciences, because she enjoyed the subject, she said, made many dear friends, and came to appreciate immensely the close "bonds of friendship" that were a feature of this small women's college. Simmons directed its students into professions, and stressed its programs in nursing, library science, and social work. Despite the school's emphasis on conventional fields for its women students, Hoare, the budding scientist, and many of her peers no doubt, had their unconventional aspirations and ambitions encouraged and nurtured. Attending a women's college, reflected Hoare, was crucial to her development as a person.

Mary Otani's parents migrated from Okinawa.[7] Her father, Saburo Yamashiro, like his elder brother, left Okinawa to avoid conscription in the Japanese army. Okinawans, Otani noted, disliked Japanese overrule of their islands. Saburo first worked as a "schoolboy," performing domestic duties and studying at a school in Honolulu, and later moved to San Francisco, where he obtained a job as a warehouse clerk in a Japanese American import business. In 1920, Otani's mother, Tsuru, joined her father in Berkeley, where a boardinghouse run by Otani's uncle served as a gathering place for Okinawans in the Bay Area. Her mother, Otani explained, was an excellent cook, and her ethnic Okinawan dishes attracted many bachelors working in the Bay Area to the boardinghouse. The six children, Fred, Henry, Mary, George, Richard, and Yoshie, grew up in Berkeley.

Berkeley was where many Japanese Americans lived, remembered Otani, because of its educational system that fed into the university. She attended Berkeley High School, and in the fall of 1941, like many of her classmates, entered the University of California. She enrolled in a general curriculum major, because, she said, there were few career options for nisei women. "I never envisioned I would be a professional," she confessed, recognizing that nisei college graduates, even those with advanced degrees, were commonly relegated to menial labor. Nisei women had fewer choices than men and were usually limited to domestic service. Indeed, Otani was a "schoolgirl," working as a domestic for her room and board while attending classes at the university. That first year and despite the war, Otani immersed herself in college life, from football games to active membership in the student YWCA. At the "Y," she recalled, she met good friends like Betty Udall, who shared an interest in race relations and social justice and action.

Before she took her final examinations in April 1942, Otani and her family were removed to Tanforan Assembly Center and then to Topaz concentration camp. In a letter to Betty Udall, she wrote of her yearning to return to the university. "You're going back to school this fall aren't you, Betty?" Otani asked in her letter of August 13, 1942. "I do wish I could go too. But my ambition is to some day go back."[8] While at Tanforan, she recalled, the Student Relocation Council sent out questionnaires to college students asking if they wanted to continue their education. She replied positively, and the Council assembled her transcript and recommendations and found a college in Arkansas that accepted her, but her papers arrived late and she missed the fall deadline. The Council next tried to place her at Grinnell College in Iowa, and finally, at Boston University.

In February 1943, Otani left the concentration camp for Boston. "I'm on the train heading on towards Omaha now," she wrote elatedly to her family on February 3, 1943. "I'm enjoying my trip very much. We got delayed one day because we missed the train at Salt Lake City. We stayed overnite at a hotel. There was nothing to get worried about as there were four of us: Mary Ono, Mits Yamada and Jim Kinoshita."[9] And she added: "There's nothing much to write as yet. I just wanted to drop you all a line so that you wouldn't get worried. Everyone's been very nice and nothing unpleasant has happened." But she noted, "We're curiosities tho' I guess." (Otani wrote to her friend Betty Udall on May 1, 1943: "I feel absolutely like a freak at times since many have never seen a Japanese before. Once in a while I get the feeling as if I were being stared at constantly.") As soon as she arrived in Boston, Otani wrote to her family to tell them of her safe arrival and her first impressions of the family for whom she would work as a domestic. From that home in Newton, Otani commuted to Boston University.

After her final examinations, Otani sat down to write a long letter to her family. Dated May 18, 1943, the letter assured her parents: "You need not worry about me at all. I'm having a wonderful time and I really like it out here. Makes me feel guilty sometimes to think that I'm enjoying myself so much when you all are stuck in such a hole. You can't imagine how *nice* everyone has been." She noted her dinner invitations, and a sleepover at a friend's home out in the country, "a wonderful place—so beautiful; there are trees and lawn and a brook, just perfect." She also reported on the "people working really hard on our problem. They've put plenty of time and effort and money to make up for something they consider unjust," she wrote of the Student Relocation Council and church groups who labored on behalf of Japanese Americans. "It really is encouraging and heartening, and I want you to be sure and realize this," she explained. "It's hard being in camp and not becoming bitter and I don't blame a single soul for being that way. I didn't realize how bitterly I felt about the whole thing and it's taken me some time to get back my perspective. You really stagnate and get barren in camp." Otani closed her letter with remembrances of beauty before the war. The lawns, shrubs, and flowers around her, she wrote, were all so beautiful. "The trees especially are just wonderful—so green and lovely. Again—the contrast between Topaz and heavenly New England. Remember the Berkeley hills? 'Tis very similar."

Several sponsors helped pay for her tuition and books, and in turn she spoke before church groups about being Japanese American and about the wartime camps. In a letter to her brother George, Otani chided him for "always telling me to shut up or keep quiet." Believe it or not, she confided, people in the Northeast paid her to speak to their group. "I got 5 dollars for speaking out in Lowell, Mass. and another 5 dollars for speaking at a Women's Christian Service Conference in Worcester . . . in front of 500 women," Otani reported. "Don't faint," she kidded her brother. "I was just as surprised as you." Still, all the while, Otani was conscious of her responsibility both to her sponsors and her fellow Japanese Americans, because she was, in the eyes of many, a representative of an entire people. I knew, she said, that "if I did well and behaved acceptably it would be possible for the other nisei students to attend [college]."

Otani's accumulating debt to others and the pressure to do well ultimately led to her decision to leave Boston University before completing her degree. She hinted at her mounting discomfort when she wrote to her family in May 1943. "In fact—too many people are concerned about me and stuff," she declared when describing her situation and telling her family not to worry about her. "Everybody's looking after me so that my life is no longer sacred."

Otani attended a YWCA "summer laboratory" from June to August 1943. There she met and interacted with students and worked on labor and social issues. The excitement of that experience contrasted sharply with her somewhat solitary life as a "schoolgirl" in the suburbs of Boston, and it gave her a taste of freedom from the debts incurred through the generosity and kindness of her educational sponsors. In a letter to her family dated July 9, 1943, she expressed her joy living and working with other students in Boston. "It's been a wonderful experience living here with all the girls!" she wrote. "I've never been so happy. . . ." The six young women worked during the day, and stayed up "every night hashing out everything." They discussed labor problems and legislation, the race riots, and racial and religious issues. "We're interested in social problems," Otani explained, "economies, legislation so that we want to cover quite a bit of material. I'm gaining so much from this group—if just the fact that I'm awfully ignorant and I have a great deal to learn."

That fall, Otani returned to Boston University with little enthusiasm, and when she wrote to her family in January, she realized that she was "getting very tired. . . . After one year of working and school I guess it would be the natural reaction," she offered, "especially since I have had very little rest in between." She could not work and study at the same time, she wrote, and thus decided to leave school after the spring semester. "I wonder if it will please you," she asked of her decision and news. Her academic interest was in sociology, but a sociology undergraduate degree was not helpful in pursuit of a career, "so I should really acquire some kind of skill so that I will be able to get a job," she reasoned. Stunted by her race and gender, leaving the university for secretarial training at a vocational school, she noted, would give her a practical skill that could help her find work. "I'm not at all sure that it is the right thing to do," she admitted. "I thought it was. But the more I think about it and the more I talk to people about it, the more uncertain I get. All I can think of is how awfully tired I get, and I get so discouraged, and I want a change."

Otani also worried about her family's prospects in the Topaz concentration camp. "Some day you all must relocate," she wrote, "there's no getting away from that. I wish that day were soon. The longer you stay in, the harder it will be to adjust. . . . I wish I really could see you again and talk this thing out." Working and "getting set," she offered, would make her independent and put her in a position to help rather than burden her family. Accordingly in May 1944, Otani left Boston for New York City and an uncertain future. "Spring is here in Boston and everything is so nice," she reported to her family on May 12, 1944. "The trees are so green; the flowers are beginning to come up; the sun is warm. Boston is a very nice city. . . . I

hate to leave it, and all my new friends. But New York seems excit-
ing and I know the experience will be good for me."

Otani's decision to leave Boston University thus originated with
her physical exhaustion and a recognition of the enormity of her debt
to others, and marked the end of her dream of a career in sociology.
She had been circumscribed and rendered dependent by racism and
sexism and the concentration camps that imprisoned her family and
impaired their economic viability and life choices. She longed for independence and freedom from obligations. "I reached a point when I
needed that," she said simply of her decision to leave Boston University. After the war and the closing of the camps, Otani returned
to Berkeley with her parents, and there, at the University of California, completed her degree in the spring of 1946.

Nisei in the Boston area, remembered Otani, formed social networks despite the injunction of the Student Relocation Council against
associating in groups to avoid undue and unwelcome attention. Men,
frequently in the military, and women, usually working or in college,
occasionally got together for parties and picnics. In fact, that was how
she met her husband. That same pattern of nisei socializing in unfamiliar and isolating environments was probably a commonplace
throughout the country. Agnes Kawate recalled nisei in the Midwest,
from Chicago, Ann Arbor, Madison, and South Bend getting together
for dances and parties. Those instances were relatively rare, however,
and her social life at St. Mary's College in South Bend, Indiana, was
less active than that of her white peers. Still, reflected Kawate, the
students, teachers, and people in the Midwest treated her well, and
she did not feel lonely.[10]

Religion was influential in Kawate's life. Born in 1924, she grew
up in a Catholic home in Turlock, California. Her mother, Fude
Yamamoto, was a Catholic in Japan, and had migrated to San Francisco as a single woman to work in the home of an American military family. Her father, Yasukazu Yamamoto, had migrated to the
United States in 1906, met Fude in San Francisco, and married her
after converting to Catholicism. The family settled in Turlock, where
Yasukazu ran a fruit-shipping business. Kawate attended the Turlock
public schools and graduated in 1942 despite the military order that
removed the family in May of that year. From Merced Assembly

Center, her family was sent to the concentration camp in Amache, Colorado.

When the Student Relocation Council announced schools open to nisei, Kawate applied to St. Mary's College. Her mother, she explained, wanted her to attend a Catholic boarding school to "be safe," and St. Mary's met her requirements. The women's college was unusual in that students, about 500 of them, wore uniforms. With few Japanese in the vicinity, Kawate felt "kind of a novelty," but there was very little hostility. Unlike Otani, who felt a keen burden of race and gender, Kawate believed that she was free of those obligations, because Midwest people did not have the race consciousness that erased her individuality. Yet, Kawate was defined by her gender and majored in sociology, because, she thought, she would help with Japan's reconstruction after the war. She ultimately went into a career of teaching after graduating in 1946. And St. Mary's, and perhaps the Midwest, were friendly but also alienating places for those who failed to fit in. There were two other nisei students during Kawate's years at St. Mary's, but both transferred before completing their degrees. One was a non-Catholic and the other moved to join her family in Chicago.

Although she lived in the Philadelphia area where groups of nisei sometimes got together for picnics and outings, Alice Matsumoto's social life revolved around her studies and work as a domestic.[11] She majored in dietetics at Temple University with few other nisei students, lived outside of the city in Bryn Mawr, and commuted to campus. Because of those circumstances, Matsumoto explained, she did not have much of a social life at the university. Still, she enjoyed the faculty and students at Temple during the one year that she was there, and completed her degree in 1944. Matsumoto was born in 1920 to Yuka Shima, a schoolteacher in Japan, and Toyoji Abe, a noted West Coast newspaper publisher and editor. She grew up in San Francisco, graduated from Lowell High School, and entered the University of California, Berkeley, in 1939. During her junior year, she met her future husband, Yoshio Matsumoto, who had transferred to Berkeley from San Diego State College in 1941.[12] They got to know each other better when both were sent to Tanforan Assembly Center, Yoshio on his own, because his parents were in San Diego, and Alice with her mother, brother, and three sisters. But they separated when Yoshio left Tanforan for Washington University in St. Louis in 1942, and Alice remained with her family until they were moved from Tanforan to Topaz. Yoshio, like Alice, graduated in 1944, and was drafted into the military. After graduating from Temple, Alice moved to New York City where she interned as a dietitian at Montefiore Hospital; and before Yoshio was sent by the Army to Germany, he and Alice met in Philadelphia and on September 14, 1945, they were married.

Social life, for George Matsumoto, was a series of overlapping circles.[13] Growing up in San Francisco and attending the University of California, Berkeley, before the war, he associated almost exclusively with fellow nisei. Although as an architectural major he worked closely with white students at Berkeley, Matsumoto had "a ball" with his mainly nisei friends. He was within half a year of graduating in 1942 when the removal orders halted his education. In Poston concentration camp, he applied to "every architectural school in the country," and was admitted to only two, Harvard and Washington University in St. Louis. He chose the latter, because he did not have the financial resources required for Harvard. At Washington University, he recalled there were lots of nisei because the doors had been opened to them. As a consequence, he had equal numbers of nisei and white friends and peers. Among his nisei friends was Yoshio Matsumoto, who was not related to him. After graduating from Washington University in 1944, Matsumoto studied for his master's degree at Cranbrook Academy of Art in Michigan, where most of the students were white women. There, he gained greater social confidence, Matsumoto said, associating with some nisei but mostly with white women.

The third-born child of Manroku Matsumoto and Iseko Nakagawa, George Matsumoto was barely sixteen years old when he entered the University of California. His overactive social life, he admitted, caused his grades to dip, but he applied himself and nearly graduated when the removals stopped his advance. The Student Relocation Council, helped him with the application process, and his stay at Poston was limited to a month. Because of his father's frozen bank account, Matsumoto had to work to support himself in St. Louis. He took a job as a "houseboy," cooking, cleaning, and gardening, but he found the work "tough." "I worked my tail off," he recalled. Believing that he was being "worked to death," Matsumoto found another job as a domestic. A Jewish couple, his second employer, had adopted a Polish refugee girl and they treated him decently, Matsumoto said. He stayed with them until he graduated. Washington University, he concluded, "gave us [the nisei] hope."

That hope for the future, any future, could not have been assumed among Japanese American youth. The mass removals and detentions tried the faith of many nisei (and issei) in American democracy and dreams of opportunities for a better life. Who could have imagined the future when the past had so starkly revealed the vagaries of life? One had to be optimistic, observed Min Yoshida, to continue one's education during the war.[14] That is why he taught mathematics to junior high school students in Topaz concentration camp, Yoshida explained, to encourage them and to restore their faith in themselves and their futures.

Min Yoshida was born in 1918, and grew up in Alameda, California. His father, Yutaro Yoshida, was born in 1879, and had migrated to America about the turn of century. He worked as a photographer in San Francisco until the great earthquake and fire of 1906, returned to Japan to marry Tome, remigrated to San Francisco, and in the early 1920s moved across the bay to Alameda, where he opened a shoe repair business. The five Yoshida children grew up and attended schools in Alameda, and the family attended the Japanese Methodist Episcopal Church. Min graduated from Alameda High School in 1937, worked for a year, and entered the University of California, Berkeley, in the fall of 1938. He majored in engineering and then business, but the wartime removals ended his Berkeley education just short of his final year.

The family remained for several months in Tanforan Assembly Center, and from there they were moved to Topaz concentration camp. Yoshida taught junior high school for about a year, and later volunteered to work in Idaho's sugar beet fields and the fields of Provo, Utah, to earn money so he could go to college to complete his degree. With the help of the Student Relocation Council, Yoshida applied to several schools that were open to the nisei and requested the necessary permits to leave the camp. He chose Dakota Wesleyan in Mitchell, South Dakota, because he could afford its tuition and it was a small, religious college in the Midwest.

Dakota Wesleyan's students and faculty, along with the Mitchell townfolk, were "very cordial" to the nisei students, Yoshida recalled, when he arrived in September 1943. He enjoyed the student discussion groups and picnics when the weather was nice, and felt that in both their academic and social life, Dakota Wesleyan's nisei were fully integrated and accepted. "What stays in my mind," he stressed, "was the friendliness of the students." During his year in Mitchell, he was concerned about his family in Topaz, but it bothered him even more that the future appeared so uncertain, not because of the disruptions of war but because of the government's treatment of Japanese Americans. The warm reception of Dakota Wesleyan's students and staff and Mitchell's residents, he noted in retrospect, was key in affirming the rectitude of his desire for an education and in restoring his confidence in American democracy and the future. In gratitude, the nisei would, long after the war's end, establish a scholarship fund for students at Dakota Wesleyan.

"I had grown up feeling secure," remembered Maye Uemura of the prewar years. "I believed in freedom, and justice, love and friendship." But the war changed everything. "It was as though the world had come tumbling down on me. I found my so-called 'friends' gathering in groups and whispering behind my back. I realized that the war had made me an instant 'enemy.'" Still, she could not have imagined that her government would remove an entire group of people in violation of their constitutional rights, take away their property and possessions, and send them to desolate camps for the war's duration. But it happened. "It made me grow up fast and think seriously about life, and what was in store for me and my family," Uemura recalled of the concentration camps. "It made me wonder about the meaning of democracy, and what I could have done to prepare myself for such an eventuality. . . . From the day the war began, I didn't know what I could depend on."[15]

Maye Mitsuye Oye Uemura was born in 1923 in Independence, Oregon. Her father, Inokichi Oye, arrived in Seattle in 1900, worked for seven years on the railroad and in lumber camps, and sent for his bride, Tao Nakamura, who joined him in Seattle in 1907. They moved to Oregon, where they farmed and where Tao had seven pregnancies but only two children survived, Maye and her older brother, Tom. The family's social life revolved around the Japanese American Christian Church, and in 1941, Maye graduated from a high school in Salem. In the fall, she enrolled at Willamette University in Salem, because it was near home and a good liberal arts school, but the war descended and with it the uncertainty spawned by blackouts and curfews, rumors, and police and FBI raids. The eviction orders came three weeks before the school year's end, but her professors fortunately allowed her to take her examinations early and thereby complete the year.

Uemura and her parents were first sent to Tule Lake concentration camp, and were later moved to the camp at Amache, Colorado in 1943. That fall, with the help of the Student Relocation Council, Uemura left camp for McPherson College in McPherson, Kansas. She chose McPherson because she felt responsible for her parents, and the college was the closest to Amache.[16] At the college, she found the students and faculty helpful and kind, but in the town where Jim Crow ruled, the nisei were classed with African Americans in their access to public facilities. After about a year at McPherson, in the summer of 1944, Uemura returned to Amache to help her elderly parents relocate to Yellow Springs, Ohio, where a group of Japanese Americans had resettled in anticipation of the closing of the concentration camps. In early 1945, to complete her undergraduate education and be near her parents, Uemura entered Ohio Wesleyan University in Delaware, Ohio, where she earned degrees in sociology and pyschology.

Her father did not want her to attend college after graduating from high school, Uemura recalled, but she wanted to continue her education and thus worked to support herself through those years. But the war tested and reinforced her resolve even more. "I was more determined than ever to complete my college education," declared Uemura, "because I felt there was so much about the world that I didn't understand. It also became clear to me that one's personal possessions could easily be taken away and would then mean nothing, but that one's thoughts and ideas could never be taken away. I needed to develop these thoughts and ideas more freely in order to begin to understand human relationships. Human relationships seemed to me basic to the understanding of society and the ills created in it."[17] The concentration camps might have broken the spirits of some inhabitants, but they strengthened the resolve of others. Education was a key to liberation.

The camps, still, created dependencies that would not have arisen ordinarily in the lives of many Japanese Americans. As government charges, they had to rely on the goodwill of others. And that reliance required a reckoning of sorts, which helped to even the balance and restore some measure of human dignity. June Kawamura remembered that she tried early on to repay her debt of gratitude for her wartime education.[18] Her father, Kenkichi Suzuki, had migrated to America during the early 1900s with a friend, and worked in the copper mines of Utah and picked the crops in many of the western states. He returned to Japan to marry Yoshi Matsuda, and settled with her in Santa Paula, California, where he worked in a packing plant. The family moved to El Monte to work as sharecroppers, and later to Los Angeles, because the schools in the rural, farming areas were inadequate. There were better schools in the city, Kawamura explained, and her parents wanted a quality education for their children, George and June. The family lived near St. Mary's Episcopal Church, and much of their social life revolved around the church. Kawamura graduated from Los Angeles High School in 1941, and in the fall entered the University of California, Los Angeles. Her first year was interrupted by the family's detention at Santa Anita Assembly Center in April 1942.

The energies of most college students at Santa Anita, Kawamura recalled, were spent trying to get out. During her six months at that race track detention camp, she wrote to obtain the necessary permissions to leave the camp and applied for admission to the University of Pennsylvania and Syracuse University. The University of Pennsylvania rejected her application on the ground that she posed a security risk at a campus where war work was being carried out, the rejection letter stated. "That made me mad," Kawamura declared, and she wrote to the Student Relocation Council to complain about the absurdity of her rejection. Meanwhile, the family was moved from Santa Anita to Gila River concentration camp in Arkansas. There, Kawamura finally received her clearances to leave but had nowhere to go. She had been accepted at Scranton Keystone Junior College, but did not want to attend a junior college and so waited for word from Syracuse. After some time, Kawamura decided that she could not delay her education any longer and accepted the Keystone offer.

Before leaving the camp, Kawamura remembered, her parents had warned her about being friendly with strangers. A young man sat next to her on the train, and tried to strike up a conversation. To his many

stions, Kawamura recalled being very formal and curt. Her com-
on persisted, telling her that he was in the military, that he had
in Hawaii, and was now on his way back home to visit his par-
He then told Kawamura that while in Hawaii he had made friends
Charlotte Shimizu from Los Angeles. Kawamura recognized
zu as her summer camp counselor, and was amazed at the coin-
e. She then proceeded to explain to the young man her situa-
d her fear about missing her transfer in Chicago. The young
vhen they arrived in Chicago, took Kawamura to her Scran-
und train, and left her there. That was the last she heard from
ung man. People, including strangers, Kawamura observed,
friendly and kind to her.
her room and board, Kawamura worked as a waitress in the
e dining hall morning, noon, and night. Between meals, she
classes. During the summer, she continued working in the
all, which catered to visiting groups, including church orga-
s that held their retreats on the Keystone campus. She was
Asian, indeed the only minority person, at this Scranton,
ania college, and people were nice but also very curious about
er reasons for being at Keystone. Church groups asked her
to them about herself and her family, Japanese Americans,
artime camps, and although reluctant at first, Kawamura even-
ed. Word spread and requests soon arrived from groups out-
llege. She was, in effect, a voice for "her people."
mistaken belief that it was a women's college, Kawamura
d to Brown University in the fall of 1944. There, she
biology because she knew a family friend, an older nisei
ho had studied biology and had gotten a job as a labora-
cian. Nisei, especially nisei women, Kawamura explained,
ly circumscribed in their career choices and those who were
at securing jobs and breaking down employment barriers
odels for their younger peers. Kawamura graduated from
946.
tude to the Episcopal Church, which had been the center
ily's social life in prewar Los Angeles and had given her
s for her wartime education, Kawamura taught for a year
ation at an Episcopal girls' school among the Sioux Indi-
th Dakota. She chose the Sioux, she said, "because they

looked like me." She also undertook a speaking tour among Episcopal church groups along the East Coast. Kawamura rejoined her parents in California in 1948, having begun the process of paying back a debt she had incurred during the war.

When Tadao Sunohara wanted to give something to his alma mater, the University of Utah, in gratitude for his education during the war, he decided on a five-foot-high bronze statue. The gift, unveiled in 1991, was a replica of the Peace Child of Hiroshima, depicting Sadako Sasaki, a twelve-year-old girl who died of leukemia a decade after the atomic bomb was dropped. Sasaki was two years old when the bomb exploded, and shortly thereafter she was diagnosed as having the "atom bomb disease." A friend told her that if she made 1,000 paper cranes, a symbol of hope, she would not die, and folded the first crane from gold paper. Sasaki made 600 cranes before dying. Her classmates folded the remaining 400, and the 1,000 paper cranes were buried with her. The statue shows the child lifting a paper crane toward the sky.

"I was born in Seattle as the son of Japanese immigrants who had come to this country in the second decade of the 1900s to seek a better way of life," Sunohara said at the dedication of his gift.[19] "However, like their peers, they soon learned that the streets of America were not paved with gold bricks and that only through the dint of hard work could they even hope to survive." They placed their future in their children's education, he continued, and it was with great joy that they learned that Sunohara had been admitted to the University of Washington for fall quarter of 1940. The wartime removals, however, brought "my long-held goal of completing college . . . to a dead stop," he said. But then college administrators and others formed the Student Relocation Council, and it helped him and other students continue their education.

"Upon learning that the University of Utah was among the early colleges to accept nisei students," Sunohara recalled, "I hastily applied for admission and was overjoyed to be accepted for the winter quarter beginning in January 1943." After eight months in the concentration camp at Minidoka in Idaho, Sunohara was apprehensive about his reception outside. "I must admit that I approached my first day on campus with some trepidation," he noted, "but, thankfully, I found that both the faculty and my fellow students were very understanding and compassionate. . . . The ensuing two years went quickly and led to my graduation in September 1944. During my studies here, I found the quality of the education I received was consistently high, and this solid education served me well in my later graduate studies and subsequent business career."

Sunohara's selection of the "Peace Child" was inspired by his deeply felt desire for world peace. "I believe that the 20th century will be viewed by historians as one of the most destructive periods in human history," Sunohara observed. "The lives of literally hundreds of millions of people have been adversely affected by wars, both hot and cold. And, thus, I believe the overriding wish of peoples worldwide is for lasting peace." His own life and that of his family had been "adversely affected" by war and hatred. His gift, "Sadako and the Thousand Paper Cranes," was in part a repayment of a debt owed to the University of Utah for its understanding and compassion. But it was also a gift of hope, like the uplifted hands of the "Peace Child," that war would nevermore disfigure the lives of humankind.

eral college campuses." At Hamilton College and Wells College in central New York, Hyer spoke with the faculty and college presidents about nisei student relocation. The Hamilton president, Hyer reported, was guarded in his response, but his Wells counterpart was "most friendly and interested" and offered to admit two nisei students and give them scholarships. "Please feel free to tell me to mind my own business if you want to," wrote Hyer to the head of the Student Relocation Council to whom she conveyed her findings. "Until you do I shall continue to at least investigate the situations in the colleges I visit."

Joe Alter, a student at Westminster College in New Wilmington, Pennsylvania, after hearing about the concentration camps, wrote to the Student Relocation Council to report his efforts to bring a nisei student to Westminster. He spoke to the college president, Al[...] informed the Council, and he "seemed interested," but wante[...] know "more facts than I could present him with. I believe tha[...] or rather we can win his support to bringing a Japanese stud[...] can persuade him that there really is a great injustic[...] of the Japanese." And Abraham Akal[...] [...]eological Seminary, inf[...]

SIX

Antiracism

THE FRAGILE TIES THAT held together the fractured lives of nisei students were more intricate than their indebtedness to fellow students and the staff and faculty members of the institutions they attended. There was a whole network of relations within that circle of circumstance and compassion. Surely there were those in government who created, in the first place, the situation of deprivation and dependency, and there were those private individuals and organizations who sought to repair the damage visited by the state on its citizens. As staff member Tom Bodine wrote in September 1943, "the Student Relocation Council has had two jobs to do during this past year and a half. Not only has it had to provide the machinery for relocation into colleges and universities, but it has also had to renew the students' faith in the American people and thus make the students *want* to relocate enough to break with their families and resist the advice of their teachers." (Some teachers had advised against a college education, Bodine noted, because they believed that a nisei was "destined to be only a manual laborer anyway.")[1]

Beyond the "machinery for relocation" provided by educational, religious, and philanthropic institutions were individuals moved by the plight and determination of nisei students. Marjorie Hyer, peace section secretary for the middle Atlantic states of the American Friends Service Committee, for example, visited colleges in her vicinity to solicit their cooperation in accepting nisei students. She was during these visits, she wrote, "poking around the officialdom on sev-

ates from concentration camp high schools into colleges and universities. The additional difficulty faced by this new group of students was a pessimism about the future bred by conditions within the concentration camps and American society as a whole. With racism so rampant and opportunities so bleak, many nisei asked, why bother with higher education when its usual rewards of upward social mobility could never by realized? "The Council's most time-consuming and challenging task," a Council publication observed, "has been to try to overcome the apathy, apprehensiveness and misconceptions that are so often a part of Relocation Center life."[4] Parents registered their concern over their children's despair. "The significance of family is now broken down," reported Rei Sakaizawa on July 7, 1943, from the Jerome concentration camp in Arkansas. "Morale is slumping sharply and character is deteriorating. No real family life is possible. . . . We do not want to keep our daughter here in the circumstance as [and?] for a job. We want her to get out of the camp and to learn how to [write] nter that growing cynicism among prospective students aff wrote more letters of encouragement and, with the financial s WCA, sel brighter side of life when everything in camp is so lousy—the food, weather, barracks, streets, recreation. . . . I know the fellows are much more depressed and disgusted than the girls. On the whole, the girls were very interested in college." Another of those returning students, Philip Nagao, reported that the most frequently asked question was, "I wonder if there's any use in going to college in this kind of circumstances?"[7]

Haruo Ishimaru, to the contrary, found attitudes at the Gila River camp in Arizona at variance with the findings of his colleagues. "There does not seem to be much apathy," he reported. "The students as a whole seem very desirous of continuing their education. Quite a few have taken the initiative to ask me what courses they should take for admittance into colleges." Parents and especially mothers, observed Ishimaru, were concerned about their daughters and their well-being on the outside. "On the whole," he concluded, "the reactions have been very wholesome, a few are apathetic but I think that it is a period of insecurity that must be dealt with by the individual with, perhaps, intelligent outside counsel."[8]

Indeed, there were as many opinions about student relocation as there were parents and prospective students. As one of the student counselors reported, "The primary reason why they [nisei high school graduates] are still in camp is parental objection and insecurity on the outside. Most of them are not interested in school; therefore, they want to go out and work, but their parents think if they do go out and work, something might happen to them." Gender played a role in that parental fear. "I have talked with parents who have said if they let their daughter out, she might run off and get married to anyone," the nisei investigator noted, "and I have talked to parents who have said if their daughter wants to go out to get married, they'll let her go, but they wouldn't let her go out to work or to go to trade school. So, each individual case is a problem within itself."[9]

The Student Relocation Council began the process of winding down its operations in the summer and fall of 1944, by transferring responsibility of college counseling to the high schools in the concentration camps. That task was formalized in November 1944, and with it the Council's staff was reduced significantly. The reduction was felt directly by students in the camps. "I was profoundly shocked to discover that within the confines of this particular Center," wrote Frank T. Inouye from Heart Mountain, Wyoming, in August 1944, "the Council was being regarded by many students as an impediment to their continuing with school. That is, correspondence with the Council's staff had been and still was, very unsatisfactory from the point of view of time elapsing between letters sent and those received, and also for the information contained, which was mostly repetitive of information sent previously, or long lists of schools which are now accepting Nisei students." That inefficiency, the nisei student counselor reported, could not be easily explained by staff reductions. If the paperwork was piling up in the Student Relocation Council offices, Inouye offered, why not retain a larger staff?

The Council's head, John W. Nason, responded to Inouye's query and criticism. He agreed that delays and inefficiency were not ideal developments. Staff reductions, however, were "a practical step which we are forced to take," Nason wrote. "We are a voluntary agency supported by contributions from private sources. The contributions have been fairly large because our work has been of considerable magnitude. The time has come when our original supporters are not prepared to continue their support on the old scale." Besides, spreading the work of student relocation to all of the camps made sense. "I would like to believe that in taking this action no one would be denied an education who might otherwise have had one," Nason stated. "Of course I know better."[10]

Because of the program's success in 1944, the following summer the Student Relocation Council sent fourteen nisei student counselors to the concentration camps under YMCA and YWCA sponsorship. This group of students had the additional responsibility of encouraging the relocation of entire families from the concentration camps to places outside. The military had removed all restrictions on colleges and universities in August 1944, and allowed the return of Japanese Americans to the West Coast in January 1945. Despite the lifting of those bans, substantial numbers of Japanese Americans remained in the concentration camps during the summer of 1945. When the war with Japan ended on August 14, 1945, about 44,000 Japanese Americans, or more than one-third of the total number confined, were still in the concentration camps.

The impending closures of the concentration camps and subsequent relocation and resettlement of families made more difficult the goal of a college education. "There are many students who are waiting to resettle their families before relocating themselves to college," a nisei counselor at the Manzanar camp reported. "Many have given up further education so that they might support the family." A nisei returnee to the camp at Minidoka, Idaho, added: "This responsibility is not necessarily an obligation to care for the family economically although in quite a few cases some degree of economic responsibility enters in. Almost always, there is the matter of taking care of the negotiations for leaving a center, finding housing and employment and looking after the many other details and transactions that are a part of resettling a family in a community. Faced with this real responsibility of taking care of aged parents who often have a language difficulty, many a boy and girl feels that his own schooling must be a secondary consideration for the time being."[11]

An early returnee to California, Esther Takei described her expectations of her summer work counseling students and their parents. She was the first nisei woman to return to Pasadena Junior College in southern California, and her arrival in early 1945 generated publicity and anti-Japanese protests. After heated debate, the complaint was withdrawn and Takei completed the school year. "The work this summer will . . . promise to be an interesting but difficult assignment," she predicted, "and will exact a tremendous amount of effort and responsibility from the returnees." Those nisei who were eager for a postsecondary education have already left the camps, she observed, and those who stayed behind "are the ones who need the most encouragement and persuasion. It is so easy," she noted, "after three long years of mental conflict and torment and heartache, for the mind to become dulled with slothful thinking and a false sense of security, and for the soul to become warped by the bitter galling touch of disillusionment and defeat. Now is the time when the need for help is the greatest. Now is the time when we must show them the road back."[12]

A few of the nisei counselors criticized and sought to distance themselves from the War Relocation Authority's method of closing the camps. When the war began, they held, Japanese Americans were wrenched from their homes and thrust into desolate wastelands, and now they would soon be forced out of secure camps and cast into the possibly hostile unknown. Instead of caring for people they had

exiled and made orphans, the government and its agency were wash-
ing their hands and absolving themselves from responsibility. "As the
time for my stay here in the center fast approaches to a close," wrote
Eugene Ueki from the Minidoka camp in Idaho, "many things have
been running through my mind. One of the first is a deep conviction
that there will be urgent need of understanding and sympathetic guidance, especially with the closing of the centers getting so near, and
with the announced intention of the WRA to get all of the people
out by all means." That eviction of people from the centers was "evacuation in reverse or a 're-kicking' of the people out of the center."
That problem of family relocation, Ueki concluded, made the project of student relocation "so small in comparison."[13]

Samuel Ishikawa was less diplomatic. "The more I stay in camp,
the more I realize the faults of the WRA policies," he wrote. "If time
permits in another report I will tell you of the 'Jap-crowism' that goes
on here in Manzanar. It is disheartening to see it come from an agency
which claims to be working for the redemption of democracy."
Ishikawa, like Ueki, was concerned about the closing of the camps
without regard to the fears or needs of the people. As a consequence,
camp residents, he noted, felt resentful toward the WRA. "They can't
understand the logic behind being herded into camp, then being forced
out," Ishikawa explained. They believed that the WRA employed
intimidation, he wrote, "to instill fear into their minds to frighten
them out of camp," and they could not understand why they were
being forced out without any prospect for housing or employment.
Even the "hot, dirty, dusty, and sultry" camp during the summer and
"cold, damp, and unbearable" camp during the winter was, by contrast, preferable to the uncertainties of life on the outside. The camp
inmate, Ishikawa declared, "simply seeks security."[14] Some of the Student Relocation Council's staff, especially those in close contact with
the nisei in the concentration camps, shared Ishikawa's critical opinion of the WRA and military.[15]

There could be no denying, nonetheless, that the Student Relocation Council was, from its inception, closely connected with the
government's War Relocation Authority. "The Council is a private
and independent agency," a Council publication noted. "It receives
no funds from the government. It does, however, cooperate closely
with the War Relocation Authority, having come into existence at the

request of that authority."[16] And insofar as it was an instrument of government policy, the WRA served the racist ends of mass removal, confinement, and redistribution. As put conservatively by the 1982 report of the presidential Commission on Wartime Relocation and Internment of Civilians, "this policy of exclusion, removal and detention was executed against 120,000 people without individual review, and exclusion was continued virtually without regard for their demonstrated loyalty to the United States." President Roosevelt signed Executive Order 9066 that authorized the exclusion, Congress enacted a law that criminalized violations of the exclusion order, and the Supreme Court ruled the exclusion constitutional within the context of war. "The personal injustice of excluding, removing and detaining loyal American citizens is manifest," the report declared.[17]

How then could the Council's work be deemed to have been antiracist? In truth, the Council's efforts to relocate nisei students were an aspect of the broader WRA mission of "relocation,"or the breaking up of prewar Japanese American communities and their scattering throughout the country. Concentrations of Japanese Americans, the reasoning held, were the cause of anti-Japanese hostility, and their dissolution would result in diminished hatreds and enhanced assimilation. Relocation was premised on the profoundly flawed proposition that racism originated with its victims and not its instigators.

Dillon S. Myer, the WRA's head for most of its existence, delineated some of the "worthwhile results" of the mass removal and detention in his "inside story" of the agency and its work. Although "unnecessary," Myer wrote, the "mass evacuation" yielded "some excellent results. . . . The most important result of the WRA program was the relocation of more than 50,000 Japanese Americans all across the United States and into the armed forces during the war period," he affirmed. "This dispersion of the population led to an understanding and an acceptance on the part of the great American public that would never have been possible otherwise. It also had a tremendous effect upon the understanding, outlook, and perspective of the Nisei in particular, which provided new opportunities and support for them and developed confidence in themselves which would not have happened otherwise."[18]

Myer explained his position during a news conference on May 14, 1943. "It would be good for the United States generally and I think it would be good from the standpoint of the Japanese-Americans themselves," he began, "to be scattered over a much wider area and not to be bunched up in groups as they were along the Coast. . . ." Relocation, he observed, helps solve "a serious racial problem by having them scattered throughout the United States instead of bunched up in three or four states." The wra's attempt at social engineering was supported, perhaps initiated, by President Roosevelt. In a memorandum dated June 12, 1944, he reflected on "this problem" of Japanese Americans returning to the West Coast after the war. For the sake of "internal quiet," wrote the president, Japanese Americans should be distributed "in many parts of the United States. . . . In talking to people from the Middle West, the East and the South," he predicted, "I am sure that there would be no bitterness if they [Japanese Americans] were distributed—one or two families to each county as a start. Dissemination and distribution constitute a great method of avoiding public outcry. Why not proceed along the above line—for a while at least?"[19]

The Student Relocation Council itself advised nisei students to avoid hanging out together, and thereby urged that they appear inconspicuous. The Asian racialized body and its ethnic culture, accordingly, were impediments to white acceptance and assimilation and had to be erased or forgotten. Mary Otani recalled that the Council instructed nisei in the Boston area to associate with Whites rather than fellow Japanese Americans,[20] and a nisei in St. Louis criticized some of his fellow nisei as "just plain drips," because "they just don't realize that they are so conspicuous when they bunch up into a group of four or five." At a residence hall cafeteria, he wrote, he and a white friend sat eating their lunch, when a nisei took a seat next to him and eventually three other nisei joined them. "I'm sure five Japanese at one table is just too much, don't you think?" he asked in exasperation.[21] Advice from the Council, thus, derived from the same "relocation" text authored by the president and wra.

And yet there was a pragmatic edge to the Council's reasoning in the matter of student relocation. The program's very existence was allowed only insofar as it met with public approval or, at the very least, tolerance. Milton Eisenhower's plan for nisei student relocation was predicated on a defensive gesture—to prevent bringing upon the program "too much opposition." The wra's first director proposed nisei student relocation, it must be remembered, at a time when "the opposition to any generosity or even decency toward the Japanese" was so vociferous in Washington, according to the Student Relocation Council's head, that even a pledge of WRA travel support for students would "endanger the entire Japanese welfare program."[22] The employment of conscientious objectors in the work of student relocation was likewise questioned on the grounds that they could "damage" the public image of the WRA.[23] Any criticism of the program, any hint of delinquency or inadequacy among nisei students might prove fatal to this great experiment. Indeed, the Council's director advised, "the more quietly we go about this [student relocation] the better, lest we fan into flame the opposition."[24]

Student relocation, in that light, was not cast from the same mold as the WRA's relocation program. While the WRA sought to engineer the assimilation and absorption of an entire people, the Council sought to foster the educational advancement of a generation. Relocation WRA style promoted self-hatred; student relocation advanced self-development. To be sure, both shared the strategy of social integration, invisibility, and the distinction between them might have been missed by some if not many; yet at base the government's plan presumed Japanese Americans to be "the problem," while the Council recognized anti-Japanese agitators as the reason, indeed necessity, for their approach. At the same time, the Council put the burden of proof, of patriotism and good citizenship, upon nisei students as representatives of an undifferentiated and racialized group. Individualism, in that sense, was a casualty of the Council's negotiation of the wider social currents of American racism.

That tension, in pursuit of an unmitigated social good amid constrained and equivocal circumstances and outcomes, was too much for some to bear. The WRA's Milton S. Eisenhower must be credited with bringing to the student relocation project the weight of the federal government, its sanction and wherewithal. Without that, the group of private citizens and volunteers who began the work of nisei student relocation could hardly have gained the degree of access they achieved to the federal bureaucracy and military that managed the concentration camps and lives and mobility of their Japanese American keep. Eisenhower was a reluctant director of the WRA, and was troubled by his assignment. "I feel most deeply that when the war is over and we consider calmly this unprecedented migration of 120,000 people," Eisenhower wrote to his former boss, Agriculture Secretary Claude Wickard, "we as Americans are going to regret the avoidable injustices that may have been done."[25]

In June 1942, after having headed the WRA for about three months, Eisenhower resigned. He had become obsessed with the WRA's task and its problems, and he had trouble sleeping at night, he confided to his friend and successor Dillon S. Myer. Perhaps the source of his discomfort arose from his recognition of the injustice of the mass removal and detention and his inability to undo the damage. "The future of the program (WRA) will doubtless be governed largely by the temper of American public opinion," he wrote in his letter of resignation to the president. "Already public attitudes have exerted a strong influence in shaping the program and charting its direction. In a democracy this is unquestionably sound and proper. Yet in leaving the War Relocation Authority after a few extremely crowded weeks, I cannot help expressing the hope that the American people will grow toward a broader appreciation of the essential Americanism of a great majority of the evacuees and of the difficult sacrifice they are making. Only when the prevailing attitudes of unreasoning bitterness have been replaced by tolerance and understanding will it be possible to carry forward a genuinely satisfactory relocation program and to plan intelligently for the reassimilation of the evacuees into American life when the war is over."[26] Intolerance among "the American people," according to Eisenhower, was the root of the problem.

Like Eisenhower, many staff members of the Student Relocation Council were deeply troubled by the "unreasoning bitterness" directed against Japanese Americans, and they took up the cause of nisei students with the intention of righting a wrong. John W. Nason was president of Swarthmore College in 1942 when he was asked to chair the Student Relocation Council's board. He accepted that challenge, he said, because he believed the mass removal and confinement was "an outrage, unnecessary, and illegal."[27] Born in 1905 in St. Paul, Minnesota, Nason grew up in Chicago, where his father made a small fortune—lost during the Great Depression—in the coal business. He attended Carleton College in Minnesota, went to Yale and Harvard for a master's degree in philosophy, and studied at Oxford as a Rhodes Scholar. In 1931 he was offered a teaching position at Swarthmore College, and in 1940 was appointed president of the college. Two years later, Nason joined the nisei student relocation effort "to correct a real social injustice" and to reintegrate nisei into American society. "This was good for our society as well as correcting an injustice," he declared.[28] Nason, whose career included a thirteen-year stint as Swarthmore's president, a post with the Foreign Policy Association, and the presidency of Carleton College, would state in retrospect, "I look upon the work that I did with the National Japanese American Student Relocation Council as the most satisfying single piece of work I've done in my career."[29]

Ann Graybill Cook, a Student Relocation Council staff member and its last director, shared Nason's assessment of his work for the Council. It was, she said simply, "the most rewarding job I ever had." And added, "it was all so very worthwhile."[30] Cook was born in 1912 in Refton, Pennsylvania. She attended public schools, and received her degree from Bucknell University in 1933. After graduating, she was alumni secretary for the middle Atlantic region's Student Christian Movement, and between 1936 and 1956 directed YWCA programs at Oberlin College, the University of Illinois, Urbana, New York University, and City College of New York. In 1945, while at the University of Illinois, Cook received a letter from her friend Betty Emlen inviting her to join her as a staff member of the Student Relocation Council in Philadelphia. At the time, Cook confessed, she hadn't known about the Council or its work, nor had she been aware of the Japanese American concentration camps. But she had known a nisei woman through her work with the YWCA, she knew about and respected the American Friends Service Committee, and was honored to have been asked by Emlen, whom she greatly admired, to join her in this work of student relocation. Although she loved her work with the YWCA, remembered Cook, Emlen's invitation "sounded like a wonderful opportunity for service that I liked and something that I could do that was positive in the wartime." So she left Urbana for Philadelphia. After serving as an assistant to the Council's board, Cook was appointed its director. The most difficult aspect of her tenure was winding down the work of the Council. It was an emotional task, she recalled, closing the office in 1946 despite knowing that the Council's job was done.

Ann Cook's friend, Betty Emlen, was born in 1919 in Cambridge,

Massachusetts, where her father was a professor at Harvard.[31] Her mother had been a professor and dean at Mills College in California before marrying. Emlen remembered her home as a place filled with stimulating guests and conversation. She attended the progressive Shady Hill School, an institution her mother helped found, and went on to Milton Academy and Vassar College. No student could leave Vassar during the late 1930s, Emlen noted, without a keen sense of social responsibility. In November 1942, she married Woodruff J. Emlen, who was a Quaker and a pacifist. Woody was born in 1913 in Philadelphia, attended Quaker schools, and graduated from Haverford College in 1935. He worked in banking for five years, and attended Harvard Business School, where he met Betty.

A week after their marriage, Woody left for San Francisco to work with the Student Relocation Committee. His draft board, he recalled, had been breathing down his neck, and service in student relocation qualified, as far as his draft board was concerned, as work "of national significance." He thus accepted the offer. Just over a month later, Betty joined him in the Bay Area, and soon both of them were involved in nisei student relocation. "The student relocation work made very good sense to me from the very beginning," remembered Betty, "and I was very thankful when we had an opportunity to be of help." Although the initial motivation was prompted by Woody's conscientious objector status, both Betty and Woody saw their labors on behalf of nisei students as important and as a cause in which they believed "so strongly." Both the project of student relocation and its beneficiaries, Betty pointed out, were mutual acts. Council staff members helped place and fund nisei students, but those students also helped themselves by pursuing their education and compiling a record of achievement. And nisei students benefited from the Council's efforts; but staff members, like Betty, gained friends, a greater appreciation of the many people of goodwill, and a knowledge of the country through its various institutions of higher learning.

Like Woody Emlen, Thomas R. Bodine joined the student relocation work because of his draft status. Born in Philadelphia in 1915, Bodine attended Quaker schools, but went to Wesleyan University because he wanted to see the world outside of Quakerism.[32] His upbringing and education, Bodine noted, were influential in shaping his convictions on pacifism, respect for persons, and social activism. He graduated from Wesleyan in 1937, and worked for four years in the insurance business in Hartford, Connecticut. In 1941, he received a draft deferment for work with the American Friends Service Committee in Philadelphia, and when the war broke out he and others were sent to the Pacific coast to monitor the situation faced by Japanese Americans. The FBI arrested and detained mainly issei leaders in the days following Pearl Harbor, the government froze their bank assets, and the military imposed curfew and travel restrictions that caused hardships upon livelihoods. Bodine went to Seattle and helped wherever he could to alleviate some of the fears and pressures prompted by the government and military.

In June 1942, the Friends Service Committee sent Bodine to San Francisco to work on nisei student relocation. He was eventually appointed the West Coast director, and he followed the office when it moved to Philadelphia. Bodine, like most of his fellow Student Relocation Council staffers, was moved by his determination to play a part in righting a great wrong, but he observed different styles among the staff that caused disagreements and rifts. Some, Bodine said, usually his "bosses," had a more bureaucratic mentality and were seemingly more concerned about numbers, raising money, and cooperating with the WRA and military than others, mainly those in daily contact with the nisei, whose primary interest was to serve the students. As an eager young man, Bodine recalled, he grew impatient with the "bureaucrats," whose approach appeared to him impersonal and forgetful of the Council's basic mission of treating students as individuals and helping them piece together their broken lives and restore their faith in America.

Bodine's field notes during his visits to the concentration camps shed some light on his emotions and motivations. "I write this from behind the barbed wire of a Relocation Camp," he began his letter to the Friends of his Germantown, Pennsylvania meeting in May 1943.[33] "Outside my window I can see the barbed wire fence and the armed guards sitting up in the watch towers. . . . I sense the evacuee's feelings of confinement, his feeling of being locked up without trial when he has committed no crime, the feeling that his country—his America—no longer considers him American. These feelings hurt. I feel for the older people, all of whom came to America more than 20 years ago. . . . These older people lived here most of their lives. They have loved America. They have helped build America. And like so many other immigrants, they have watched their children become real Americans." It "hurts," he continued, to talk to college-age youth who are uncertain about their futures. "It hurts to be here, but it helps to share that hurt with some of you on the outside who happen to read this," he concluded.

Those acts of charity by Whites were, as Betty Emlen observed, reciprocal and reciprocating. They were not simply given; they were enjoined and returned. Kay Yamashita was just one of the many nisei who assisted in and advanced the work of student relocation.[34] Born in Oakland, California, Yamashita was the sixth of seven children, and remembered her early years as filled with warmth and love. Although a child of the Depression, she said, her childhood was very rich indeed. Yamashita graduated from University High School, went to the University of California where she planned to go into social work, and graduated just before the war. When the eviction orders were issued, her family was sent to Tanforan Assembly Center, but Yamashita was given a travel document to testify at a trial in Washington, D.C., in the company of her mother.

When they returned to the Bay Area, Yamashita recalled, she was amazed to find a group of people active in the work of student relocation. Her travel document allowed her and her mother to stay out of the camp, until a suspicious person informed the police and had her mother put in jail. Yamashita had been away at the time, and when she appeared at the police station with their travel pass, she gained her mother's release. Her mother, however, had had enough of "freedom" by that time and thus entered Tanforan to rejoin her family. Yamashita remained outside and worked for student relocation, going in and out of Tanforan to recruit students and bring from the outside books and supplies needed in the camp. She was, she said, a "gal out of captivity." She eventually joined her family in Tanforan and moved with them to the concentration camp at Topaz, Utah, because the family wanted to stay together especially with the future so uncertain.

At Topaz, Yamashita resumed her student relocation work and set up an office in the camp. Tom Bodine visited her there, and urged her to join the Student Relocation Council in Philadelphia, which she did after having spent about two months in Topaz. That experi-

ence of living in the camp, Yamashita reflected, was crucial in helping her truly understand and appreciate the plight of the nisei. When
she arrived in Philadelphia in the fall of 1943, she found a committed and hardworking staff that included Betty and Woody Emlen,
Trudy King, and Tom Bodine. The staff, she recalled, "impressed me
so much," and their example was both "heartwarming and overwhelming." She remembered the government's bureaucracy as "unfor-
giving," but discovered so many compassionate and kind people who
helped the nisei find the courage and means to leave the camps and
pursue their education.

Yamashita, too, exhibited a fierce dedication to her labor of love
and possessed a benevolent spirit that permeated her letters to students. Vickie Hata's name came to the Council's attention through
Toru Matsumoto, who was a minister of the Reformed Church and
a member of the Committee on Resettlement of Japanese Americans.[35]
Matsumoto, in his travels, met Hata when she was a student at
Emmanuel Missionary College in Berrien Springs, Michigan. Hata
was from Hawaii and a student at Whittier College in California, when
the war came and she was placed in detention. She managed to relocate to Emmanuel but found the college inadequate in sociology, her
desired major. Consequently, recounted Matsumoto, Hata sought
admission to Swarthmore or Oberlin, hoping to transfer. "Won't you
write her and give your advice?" Matsumoto asked the Council's Betty
Emlen. "She is a very fine girl, and any college that will receive her
will be very fortunate, I think."

With that lead, Kay Yamashita wrote to Vickie Hata. "I am
delighted to have this opportunity to write to you," Yamashita began,
"and hope I can be of some assistance to you." What followed was a
detailed, two-page, single-spaced typed letter outlining Hata's options
for transfer and a commentary on which institutions were particularly strong in sociology. "I could suggest to you any number of
schools," Yamashita explained, "but I believe your problem is this—
you might ask yourself these questions, what kind of school do you
wish? Do you wish a super school well known for its sociology department, or do you wish a grade A liberal arts school offering good courses
in sociology? Do you plan to go on to graduate work?" She could be
of more help, Yamashita told Hata, if she knew "exactly what was in
your mind and what your future plans were." And, she concluded,

"I do look forward to receiving a letter from you suggesting ways in which we can be of more assistance to you."[36]

Just over two weeks later, Hata responded to Yamashita. "It was with great interest and appreciation that I read your letter," began a grateful Hata. "When it came, I meant to have answered you right away because I was very impressed at your sincerity." She studied Yamashita's letter, Hata continued, and thought things over carefully, and decided to remain in the Midwest to be near her friends. "Probably to you this reason is silly," offered Hata, "but to me, it means so much." She would be going to Drake University in Des Moines, Iowa, Hata told Yamashita, because her brother was there and because it was in the Midwest. "Thank you for all you have done for me," wrote Hata. "I hope to study in the East [for graduate work] if plans work out that way."[37]

"I was very happy to hear from you and to know that you have already decided to go to Drake University," Yamashita replied. "I have no doubts that you will like the school as we have had only glowing reports about the friendliness and cordiality of the campus." Yamashita continued advising Hata and reassuring her that she had made the correct decision. For social services work, Yamashita noted, one's undergraduate degree was probably not very important except that it come from an accredited school. And she empathized with Hata. "You may be interested to know that I, too, am having a difficult time in making a decision . . . and I find myself so attached to the East Coast that I somewhat dread the idea of returning West. People and your association with them make all the difference in the world," observed Yamashita. "We all send you friendly greetings and best wishes for a very pleasant semester at Drake University."[38]

There were other Japanese Americans who aided the work of student relocation. Ken Yamamoto and Nao Takasugi were employed in the offices of the Student Relocation Council in Philadelphia. Helen Aihara, a student who was helped by Grace Nichols and Marian Lind, teachers at the Poston concentration camp, returned the fifty dollars they had given her by sending that amount to the Student Relocation Council for use in its work. "The enclosed money order is being sent to you as a request from Grace Nichols and Marian Lind," wrote Aihara to the Council. "Their loan made possible so many fine things for me. I am repaying them by sending you the money they gave me.

With a hope that it will help another."[39] A nisei soldier, who had been helped by the Council before his induction, set aside a portion of his monthly salary to benefit a nisei woman student selected by the Council. He called it the "K.O. Fund for the O.K. Girl." And many Japanese Americans within the camps raised money from among themselves for student scholarships. At Topaz concentration camp, the Topaz Student Aid Fund raised $3,196 from among the internees and thereby helped thirty-one students attend college. "We gave $100 to each student to get started," the chairman of that fund explained. "It was not the amount of money they received, but it was the spirit of encouragement which was given to them that caused them to fight for higher education."[40] There were similar funds at Heart Mountain, Gila, Poston, and Tule Lake concentration camps. Even nisei students, like those in the St. Paul-Minneapolis area, contributed money to the Student Relocation Council.[41] All of those efforts were generous to a fault, especially because most of the Japanese Americans within the camps were unemployed, and those without were barely scraping by.

In truth, the overall project of nisei student relocation during World War II was a mutual endeavor by both benefactors and the recipients of their goodwill. This was not a single-directional act of charity one to another. Whites came to the aid of their fellow Americans who had been rendered dependent by the state. They sought to right a terrible wrong. But Japanese Americans, too, helped in that effort of restoring faith in themselves, their fellow citizens, and their government. White Americans were enriched by the experience; they gained lifelong friends, job skills, and contacts. Japanese Americans were similarly endowed, and in the process aided in the education of a generation of students who might have otherwise been irreversibly stunted in their development.

Ultimately, it was American democracy that benefited from this mutual struggle against racism, not in the narrow sense of saving a generation from a self-absorbing bitterness, but in its widest meaning of restoring the freedoms and rights of a people that had been foreclosed by racism's illiberal role. Democracy's promise was the beneficiary of this antiracist cause. Surely that is the central lesson of the nisei student experience—the soul-searching challenge and responsibility of living in a democracy. The Constitution is a mere "scrap of paper," as Assistant Secretary of War John J. McCloy expressed it in

1942 when defending the plan for Japanese American removal and detention.[42] In that sense, the Constitution is lifeless; people animate it, give it life. And our freedoms are guaranteed only when we the people act to resolve threats to them.

But there are also other lessons derived from this experience. The definitions of membership in the American community and therewith rights and privileges are subjects of contestation and recurrent struggle. In the case of prewar America, various lines demarcated citizenship and liberties, including statutes that disenfranchised Asian immigrants and restricted naturalization to Whites and Blacks, and social practices that circumscribed access and opportunities based upon race, gender, and class. Nisei students were, at the very least, U.S. citizens by birth and thus possessed some basis for making claims, but even this was rendered spurious by the fact of the concentration camps that failed to distinguish between alien and citizen. To the state, Japanese Americans were, as a "race," without distinction.

Concerned Whites—educators, students, religious folk, philanthropists, politicians—for whatever reason, sought to restore to some nisei limited community membership, but these were those who had compiled a record of academic achievement and good citizenship and who had been cleared by the FBI as being safe for democracy. This was a select group. As of May 1, 1946, the Student Relocation Council had on file, according to Kay Yamashita, the names of 3,613 students at 680 institutions. The Council closed its doors on June 30, 1946.[43] Although not inclusive of all nisei students, the Council's files represented only about six percent of the total population of nisei. Even after their selection as members of that chosen class, nisei students faced limited options because of induced economic constraints that precluded a college education for some and determined which schools were affordable for others. Their choices were further reduced by military restrictions that loosened over time, but proved nonetheless influential in sending nisei to numerous small colleges in far off places to which they would not have ordinarily gone. Those deterrents no doubt affected nisei life choices and careers after their graduation. Women carried the added responsibility of caring for aged parents in the concentration camps and were hindered by parental fears of a hostile outside world for women beyond the barbed wire enclosures and by patriarchal dictates that directed them, for the most part, into selected courses and careers.

The nisei student experience, I believe, points not only to a neglected area in the much-studied topic of Japanese Americans and World War II, but also to a slighted subject matter in Asian American Studies broadly—the nature and consequences of antiracism. What the historian Herbert Aptheker has observed of American history has validity for Asian American history as well. "It is certain— indeed, painfully obvious—that racism has permeated U.S. history both as idea and practice," wrote Aptheker. "Nevertheless, it always has faced significant challenge." Antiracism among Whites, he holds, "has been significant beginning in the colonial epoch and continuing through the twentieth century."[44] Like the literature on race in American history, white racism has been the dominant concern and object of analysis in Asian American history. Beginning generally with the agitation against the Chinese during the nineteenth century, that history recounts in great detail and in numerous volumes the deeds of white people against successive migrations of Chinese, Japanese, Koreans, Asian Indians, and Filipinos. And yet, the deeds of Whites (or African Americans or Latinos) against anti-Asian racism have not been recorded in a systematic way or deployed as a major analytic construct within considerations of the American racial formation. Those failures, I believe, exemplify both the hold of racism on our imagination and the need for a more thoroughgoing, critical examination of Asian American (and U.S.) historiography. They also reveal some far-reaching consequences that impair historical understanding, such as perceiving Whites and Asians as undifferentiated masses devoid of individuality and diversity and as rendering the past without tension or resolution between oppression and resistance. Where there is racism, Aptheker reminds us, there is opposition. Asian American Studies must move beyond the bounds of racism as its organizing principle to interventionist practices that defy those conventions of race.

The essential question for this book, I suppose, is the nature of antiracism and its articulations with racism and their outcomes. Surely they define one another, racism and antiracism, and as the example of nisei students shows, antiracism can never be a one-way process of Whites bestowing liberty's gifts upon Asians. It is a collaborative project. And even as racism is inseparable from sexism and homophobia, antiracism must engage those allied and synergetic forms of oppression. Antiracism can also never be an entirely wholesome and unmixed good. Like racism, it is situated in time and place and freighted with multiple meanings, ambiguities, and contradictions because of its complex and portable social positions and contexts. Education might have enabled careers, but it also shunted nisei students into prescribed tracks as Japanese American and as men or women. Relocation was a strategy designed to minimize anti-Japanese opposition, but it also sought to disperse communities and dissipate an ethnic culture. There is ample cause for celebration and mourning in this story of nisei students.

Although racism's reach is at least as long as America's past, antiracism's counter bequeaths a similar legacy. Lafayette Noda, a nisei student during the war, wrote to E. C. Adams, editor of the *Livingston Chronicle,* in response to articles published in the paper during the summer of 1943. Displaced on the East Coast, Noda remembered his home in California. "Livingston shall always be remembered for happy childhood memories, but mostly for the enjoyable times had in work and play with many others from whom we have become separated," Noda began. Those "times made precious" were filled with companionship "as we stood in our Scout uniforms to salute the flag, went on trips together, played ball, debated, greeted friends in the streets, sweated together in the same fields or orchards at harvest time, and went together to church to pray to the same God." The war might have changed that, continued Noda, separating those companions, Whites from Japanese Americans. Yet the basic humanity of Japanese Americans remained, and the ideals of American democracy still required adherence. "God grant that all of us may continually seek to live up to those ideals!" Noda declared. "May we evacuees never grow bitter or show hatred but work ever with the faith that it is as we live and work together that we strive toward the ideals we profess."[45] Decades later, in 1980, Noda was one of the leaders in establishing the Nisei Student Relocation Commemorative Fund as a tribute to the work of the wartime Student Relocation Council by helping Southeast Asian students, displacements of war, pursue higher education. The Fund was also formed to promote cross-cultural understanding "as we live and work together," in Noda's words, and "strive toward the ideals we profess." The work of antiracism generated by World War II is being carried on into the present by the nisei and their children.

When Kiyo Ogawa approached the threshold of graduation in May 1945, she wrote to Betty Emlen of the Student Relocation Council. "As I look forward to graduation and the work which lies before me, I cannot help but share my happiness and the things which have made it possible for me to complete my college work," she reflected. "If it was not for your council's interest in us [the nisei], I am certain that many of us would have faced many problems. . . . I cannot launch into my field without feeling and knowing that you had a definite part in making my career possible. I am indeed indebted to you. . . . Tho' the future may be uncertain, it is a challenge for me, as an American, to be a part of the country in which I am proud to live, learn, and take part in building for true Democracy. . . . Words fail me, but I trust you will accept my humble, but sincere and grateful heartfelt appreciation."[46]

Nearly fifty years after Ogawa wrote her letter, Betty Emlen explained to me why she had solicited money to aid students like Ogawa. "If you believed in something so strongly," she said, "I didn't feel embarassed to ask anybody because I felt it was so important." And while Ogawa might have admired Emlen for her labors on her behalf, Emlen was in awe of nisei students like Ogawa. "I just marvelled at why some of these topnotch students who had to leave university or college in the middle had the courage to start in again," Emlen declared. "They were really dedicated. With that kind of motivation, why wouldn't you ask whoever you could to provide for them. Why wouldn't you work six days a week" for that cause? In fact, Emlen noted, those who helped nisei students weren't all that significant. Rather, "we thought it was important that these people should get an education." The concentration camps represented a terrible waste of talent. The education of the nisei, Emlen concluded, "was good for the United States as well as for the Japanese Americans." The debt, in truth, has been paid in full, many times over.

AFTERWORD

Nisei Student Relocation
Commemorative Fund

Leslie A. Ito

One warm June evening in 1996, thirteen Southeast Asian high school graduates received college scholarships for their academic excellence. These students from Brooklyn, Queens, and the Bronx were not only graduating in the top ranks of their classes, but were also involved in numerous extracurricular activities, including student government, the yearbook, the Vietnamese Culture Club, and various athletic teams, to name just a few. Many also volunteered with social service organizations, showing their dedication to the Southeast Asian community and humanity at large. This distinguished group of students through hard work and perseverance were able to overcome poverty, linguistic and cultural barriers, and the post-traumatic stress of war, and yet they managed to achieve academic and extracurricular success. Proud parents and friends joined the celebration and observed the students as they received scholarships to help continue their education.

This was not a traditional scholarship award ceremony, nor was it sponsored by an educational institution or a corporation. It was sponsored by the Nisei Student Relocation Commemorative Fund, and among the awardees and their families sat a dozen or so nisei men and women who had received similar opportunities to go to college during World War II. This Japanese American group and their peers nationwide formed this scholarship fund specifically for Southeast Asian students to carry on the legacy of goodwill and opportunity for higher education. Chiyo Moriuchi, the treasurer of the Fund, closed her presentation at the ceremony with a statement that captures the Fund's essence: "Tonight we commemorate the past, celebrate the present and renew our commitment to a brighter future for all Americans."[1]

The history of the Commemorative Fund began in 1976, when the

Japanese American Citizens League (JACL) hosted a conference in San Francisco on nisei retirement. The JACL chose fifty representatives from across the nation to attend. Among those selected was Nobu Hibino from Portland, Connecticut, who was then working in the low-income housing sector. Hibino was a graduate of Lowell High School in San Francisco, and attended the University of California, Berkeley. World War II and America's concentration camps suddenly interrupted her college education in the second semester of her senior year. She and her family were removed from their home and sent first to Tanforan Assembly Center and later to the concentration camp at Topaz, Utah.

Hibino's involvement in promoting higher education began at Tanforan, where she worked in the high school guidance office. During the summer of 1943, the National Japanese American Student Relocation Council (NJASRC) hired her to work at their headquarters in Philadelphia. Hibino and her two brothers received assistance from the NJASRC, and she completed her degree at Boston University but received her diploma from Berkeley. Through her work with the Relocation Council, she became acquainted with the staff who helped her settle in the Boston area. Trudy King of the NJASRC graciously let Hibino use her apartment in Cambridge while she attended Boston University.[2]

After completing her degree in Boston, Hibino remained there to marry and raise her family. Thus, because of her geographical location and her community involvement, she represented the New England area at the JACL conference on retirement and was expected to conduct a similar conference for the nisei in her area. But when she returned to Massachusetts, she faced some difficulties in fulfilling her obligation. At that time no nisei groups existed in New England. Hibino searched for nisei through the Boston phone book and through the JACL mailing lists. A few months following the JACL conference, after great effort, she organized the New England Nisei Retirement Conference, held at Boston University.

Twenty-four nisei, traveling from as far as Rhode Island, Connecticut, Maine, and New Hampshire, attended this gathering. Although many believed that discussions of retirement were premature, most were interested in sharing their stories and creating a common bond. For many, this event was the first time they had been in the company of such a large group of Japanese Americans since their wartime detention.

The conference resulted in many friendships as well as social networks. The group became known informally as the "New England Nisei," and began meeting for annual picnics and an *Oshogatsu* celebration for the New Year. Attendance grew at the annual gatherings, and the group decided that they needed to formulate a more constructive and meaningful reason to meet. They discussed their reasons for residing on the East Coast, and realized that many shared a common history. Not only had they all been held in the concentration camps, but many shared the experience of going to college during the war years and benefiting from the help of the National Japanese American Student Relocation Council. That realization led to discussions of establishing their own scholarship fund to continue the legacy of fighting against racism through higher education. Among those in attendance that day were Lafayette Noda and Nobu Hibino, both former employees of the Student Relocation Council.[3]

Lafayette Noda was attending the University of California, Los Angeles, when the Japanese bombed Pearl Harbor. He was confined at Heart Mountain, Wyoming, and later at Amache, Colorado. While in camp, he was admitted to Swarthmore College to finish the work for his degree. During his stay in Pennsylvania in 1944, he volunteered with the Quakers and Student Relocation Council, although he had never received direct assistance from the Council.[4] After completing his doctoral degree in 1957, Noda became a professor of biochemistry at Dartmouth College, where he remained until his retirement. His involvement with the Student Relocation Council prompted him to actively support the proposal for a student scholarship fund.

After months of planning, in 1980 the New England Nisei group launched the Nisei Student Relocation Commemorative Fund. Many of the nisei students' sansei (third-generation Japanese American) children have also become active in the organization. The New England Nisei formed the fund in tribute to those who assisted them during World War II in similar situations, a concept of reciprocity stemming from the Japanese-idea of *on-gaeshi*, repayment of a moral debt.[5] The Commemorative Fund's slogan, "Extending Helping Hands Once Offered to Us," clearly states both its commemorative and philanthropic objectives. The board of the scholarship fund deserves much credit for volunteering endless hours to keeping the scholarship contest program operating for over two decades in order to pass on this opportunity for a higher education.

In June 1982, the Commemorative Fund presented the first financial grant to the American Friends Service Committee in Philadelphia. This Quaker organization played a large part in spearheading, organizing, and volunteering with the National Japanese American Student Relocation Council. Had it not been for the Quakers, many of the nisei students believe they would not have had the opportunity to continue their education. Not only were the Friends contributors to the wartime Council, but they continued to lend leadership and administrative support. Among those recognized were John W. Nason, former president of Swarthmore College, and staff members Betty and Woody Emlen, Robert O'Brien, Thomas Bodine, Ann Graybill Cook, Trudy King Toll, and Bill Stevenson.[6] With the Fund's grant of $2,000, the Quaker organization sponsored a symposium in Boston on racial issues. Thus began the next cycle of reciprocity through goodwill and education.[7]

The Commemorative Fund's board decided that in the following years the Fund should seek "to aid and uplift poor and underprivileged Pacific Asian racial minorities in the United States by providing scholarships to attend universities and colleges and training schools and programs."[8] The board recognized that Southeast Asian refugees faced a plight similar to that of Japanese American students during World War II, and designated the scholarship specifically for Southeast Asian students who were college-bound. The Commemorative Fund is unique in crossing ethnic boundaries and creating a greater sense of pan-Asian unity.

The Fund serves two purposes: to foster optimism among Southeast Asian high school graduates and offer them academic scholarships, and to commemorate those who dedicated themselves to help the nisei students during World War II. Specific funds are created in memory of influential figures who participated in the student relocation movement and also to remember the many nisei students who have passed away. Since its inception, the Fund has grown from just a few thousand dollars to over $300,000. In 1990 and 1991, it increased significantly as a result of the successful campaigning by the Philadelphia and Seattle committees. Also at this time, nisei began receiving their redress money from the U.S. government under the Civil Liberties Act of 1988 and many graciously donated it to the Commemorative Fund.[9]

Partly in response to the influx of Southeast Asian immigrants and their dispersal across the country through resettlement programs, the annual scholarship contest rotates to various regions in the United States where there are significant Southeast Asian communities. Each city forms its own pan-ethnic scholarship committee and relies on the Southeast Asian community organizations for further outreach. This is the only scholarship fund specifically established for Southeast Asian college students. Criteria for the selection of winners are based on personal and academic qualifications, educational objectives, and financial need.[10]

The scholarship contest began in San Francisco in 1982. Kenji Murase, professor of social work education at San Francisco State University and the chair of that year's committee, set the format for the following years' selection process and the scholarship program. In subsequent years, the scholarship contest traveled to Chicago, Los Angeles, Minneapolis–St. Paul, Houston, Denver, Philadelphia, Seattle, Boston, Stockton, Sacramento, Fresno/Tulare, New York City, and San Diego.[11]

By following the Student Relocation Council's example, the Commemorative Fund has sought to help Southeast Asian students obtain a college education and nurture hope for a brighter future. Nobu Hibino, the Fund's executive secretary, described the parallel between the two student groups: "It's the same because we were forced to leave our homes. They were forced to leave for political reasons." She also described the differences between the two groups: "Whereas most Japanese Americans were U.S. citizens fluent in English, many Southeast Asians had to survive treacherous conditions to arrive in this country. Once here, they had to learn the culture and the English language." Beyond the language barriers, many Southeast Asian refugees were permanently separated from their families once they reached the United States.[12] Both student groups experienced the trauma of war, yet both had a passion for learning and the desire to strive for a better future through education.

Although war affected both groups of students, the Southeast Asians also witnessed the violence and terror of warfare. Most of the

Commemorative Fund's awardees and their families who escaped Vietnam, Cambodia, and Laos were victims of both the Vietnam War and the harsh impact of communism. On March 1975, after nearly two decades of American involvement in Vietnam, communism overtook Saigon and spread across Indochina. At that time, President Gerald Ford allowed approximately 130,000 Southeast Asian refugees into the United States and established the Interagency Task Force to administer resettlement. Later that year, Congress passed the Indochina Migration and Refugee Assistance Act, which funded the resettlement of Southeast Asian refugees. The federal government compensated states for the social services and assistance they provided for the refugees. That first wave of 130,000 refugees consisted primarily of educated professionals and government and military officials and their families.[13] In 1975 and 1976 nearly 65,000 Southeast Asian children, or 42 percent of the refugees, were under the age of eighteen, thus having the largest impact on the public schools in areas of major Southeast Asian concentrations.[14]

Those programs included classes to teach English language and job skills, as well as secondary and primary education.[15] However, the government gave minimal assistance for higher education. Like the nisei students, the Southeast Asian college-bound youth had to find their own means for a college education. Furthermore, the college admissions process categorized these refugee students as Asian American, thus often regarding them as a "model minority" and overlooking their unique circumstances. In reality, those students did not fit an elitist academic stereotype but were from families of low socioeconomic status, possessed limited English skills, and had experienced the trauma of war.[16]

The more recent Commemorative Fund awardees were part of the second wave of refugees. After the Vietnam War had spread into Laos and then to Cambodia, thousands of Cambodians, Chinese Vietnamese, ethnic Lao, Mien, and Hmong fled to America in search of political refuge. This new group reached its peak with 150,000 refugees seeking protection in the United States in 1979, the same year that the New England Nisei began planning the Fund. The second wave was more diverse socioeconomically, including people less educated and urbanized than the first group.[17]

In 1980, while the Commemorative Fund was still in the planning stage, the United States enacted the Refugee Act to provide protection for refugees and their families. The United Nations definition of a refugee is "any person who, owing to a well-founded fear of being persecuted for reasons of race, religion, nationality, membership of a particular social group or political opinion" seeks refuge in another country. Under that law, the immigration quota was raised to 50,000 refugees, a system of admission was instituted, Congress and not the executive branch was given power to regulate refugee policies, and most important, the U.S. promised to provide asylum and finance resettlement.[18]

As was the case in Vietnam, the spread of communism displaced thousands of refugees from Laos and Cambodia. For many of the college-aged students, those memories of oppression and survival were driving forces in their educational pursuits. Seng K. Suy, one of the 1990 Philadelphia winners, recalled the horrors of his life in Cambodia, where he was forced to work at gunpoint. Although conditions have improved for Suy and his family in America and starvation is no longer an issue, they continue to face poverty. Suy observed, "All my life I grew up knowing only poverty. I want to see life beyond poverty. The only way I can beat poverty is through a good education."[19] Suy graduated first in his class at University City High School.

Another Philadelphia winner in 1990 and Suy's Cambodian classmate, Sapheap Sak, recounted his experiences under the communist Khmer Rouge. "In the Khymer Rouge Camp I was forced to work from six in the morning to six in the evening without eating breakfast or getting paid," he recalled. Sak was separated from his parents for two months during this time. Every evening he witnessed the Khmer Rouge choose innocent victims to be killed in the forest. Fortunately, his family was saved, but they endured a great deal of pain. Sak continued: "When I think back I want to cry. I become stronger from the experience and realize how lucky I am to be here in the United States. I have confidence in myself, knowing that I can become whatever I want."

The Fund also helps students realize that there are people who believe in them and who are working to reverse discrimination. Leark Vath was a 1993 award recipient who attended the University of California, San Diego. Vath and his family immigrated to the United

States in 1980 from Cambodia. His father was ill and thus unable to work. Vath, his brother, and father survived on an annual income of less than $6,000. When Vath graduated from Modesto High School, he knew that to attend college he would have to find financial assistance. By the time he graduated, Vath had received over $1,800 in scholarship grants including the Commemorative Fund's award. "The award really inspired me to go to college and gave me a new found sense for humanity because since I came to the U.S., I had always thought of this country as nothing but a bunch of greedy people. I know this society is solely based on money, but now I know there are people out there that really care for people like me."[20] With his scholarship money, Vath was able to support himself.

Not only did Vath secure an educational future through his scholarships, but he was able to become financially independent from his family. "By not being a burden on my family made me feel good and I owe this to the NSRCF," he noted. Vath anticipates graduating in the spring of 1998 and working for a securities brokerage firm. He aspires to become part of a "financial crusade" to help families learn how money works, helping them get out of debt and achieve a brighter financial future.

Those Southeast Asian students, like the nisei students during World War II, have strong ties with their communities and carry the responsibility of representation of and accountability to their people. Many of the personal essays written by the scholarship applicants exhibit that strong sense of group identity. Huan N. Phan, who graduated from Blackford High School in San Jose and attended the University of California, Berkeley, was one of the 1983 Commemorative Fund recipients. Phan is concerned with providing guidance to Southeast Asian youth. From his experience as a Vietnamese political exile, he realizes the difficulties of maturing within a new culture and the conflicting values between the old and new cultures. Phan hopes to help Southeast Asian children develop strong self-esteem and a pride in their culture. He wrote: "By teaching the youths of my ethnic origin about their rich heritage, I will provide the young generation with a solid foundation upon which self-discovered identities can develop."[21] Phan carries on the nisei World War II tradition of student "ambassadorship" and mentorship through his commitment to his community.

Giving back to one's community continues to be a theme for many of the Commemorative Fund's recipients. Mayna Moua, a 1993 Hmong awardee at the University of California, Davis, with a dual degree in human development and psychology, said: "With this, I plan to get my teaching credentials and help influence young children to get a higher education and work to help the community."[22] Moua's family were thankful and overjoyed that their only daughter was able to attend college with the help of the Commemorative Fund.

Like many Japanese Americans, large numbers of Southeast Asian refugee families have a strong commitment to education as a means to socioeconomic advancement in America. Refugee families make large sacrifices for their children's education in hopes of a better life. For the older Southeast Asians, the next generation with their college degrees is their only hope for social improvement.[23] Christine Tan, award recipient from Stockton, arrived in the United States in 1984. The Tan family's main motive for coming to America was to obtain "a good education and to build a better life." She recalls how her parents stressed the importance of education. "They told me that only education can bring me happiness and a bright future," Tan remembered.[24] With education as a priority, Tan studies to be a pharmacist.

The parents of some students, like Hanh Kim Nguyen, remain in Asia. Nguyen arrived in the United States in 1987 with her two younger brothers, and her parents stayed in Vietnam with her four younger siblings. Although she misses her parents greatly, she reminds herself, "I feel I am a very lucky person. I have the opportunity to obtain an education in America. I wouldn't have had the chance to do so if I had stayed in Vietnam." In this case, not only was Nguyen's education a sacrifice for her family still in Vietnam, but it was also the personal sacrifice for her of being separated from her parents and other siblings.[25]

By receiving a college degree, some students believe that they can overcome economic inequality and racial and gender discrimination. Kim-Vinh Nguyen, who arrived in the United States in 1975 with her mother and three siblings, remarks: "Being both a woman and a racial minority, I have seen and felt the kind of discrimination that has prevented women and peoples of color from pursuing higher education and achieving their aspirations. That experience is a major factor in my decision to further my education."[26] Nguyen was one of the 1983 Fund winners from Berkeley High School.

With educational opportunities and encouragement from the Nisei Student Relocation Commemorative Fund, these refugee students are able to achieve their dreams. Because of increasing university tuition fees, the financial support from the Fund is greatly appreciated. Furthermore, a close bond has been formed between the award recipients and the regional members of the Commemorative Fund. Many of the students keep in close correspondence with the Fund throughout their years in college. Jenny Chang, a 1993 Stockton winner, from Modesto, California, writes: "The background of the nisei fund and the existence of this scholarship program served to affirm and strengthen my views that an education, especially a higher one, is surely not a given but a privilege." Chang arrived in the United States in 1980. She was active in community and civic affairs, and graduated valedictorian of her high school class. The Commemorative Fund's recognition of Chang's achievements and academic promise provided her with confidence and encouragement to acquire a college education.

Many of the letters from the Fund's recipients echo the gratitude that the nisei students showed the Student Relocation Council staff and volunteers. For young scholars like Sean Yan, a 1990 winner from Philadelphia, the Fund helps educational dreams come true. Before his arrival in the United States, he had never been allowed to attend school, because in Cambodia he was forced into slave labor when he was eight. Yan escaped the labor camp and spent a week living on wild vegetation and sleeping in trees to protect himself from preying animals. Once reunited with his family, they tried twice to escape to the Thai border. After successfully arriving at a Thai refugee camp, they went to Indonesia and eventually settled in West Chester, Pennsylvania, with uncles of Yan's brother-in-law.[27]

For Yan, educational opportunity was a blessing and a formerly unattainable luxury. Thus he strives to do his best every day and is always looking for more learning opportunities. Yan graduated second in his high school class at Roxborough High School. He notes: "I am thrilled that there are organizations such as this one, which offer opportunities to young dreamers such as I am. I know I have the ability, but I need the opportunity."[28]

These students realize that their dreams of freedom and opportunity in America can be clouded by racial discrimination. Yet, with the mentorship and financial assistance of the Nisei Student Relocation Commemorative Fund, these Southeast Asian students have help in achieving their goals to become leaders of their community and carry on the legacy of the student relocation movement and those who made higher education for the nisei possible.

Over fifty years have passed since World War II and the detention of Japanese Americans, yet social, economic, and educational inequalities and prejudices still occur in our society today. Many Asian Americans experience that discrimination, particularly the Southeast Asian refugees. These eager young students dream of pursuing a college education, but because of their socioeconomic status, their visions are shattered. Much like nisei college students during World War II, Southeast Asian students see a college education as a vehicle to achieving economic success and social equality. The former nisei students recognize that vision, and the frustrations of not being able to reach those goals because of economic and political circumstances. They thus created the scholarship fund to help Southeast Asian refugees obtain a college education.

The National Japanese American Student Relocation Council and those who assisted the Japanese American college students in their relocation to Midwest and East Coast campuses helped rebuild the esteem and morale of this group of nisei. With a renewed, more positive outlook on life and the knowledge and training acquired in college, many of those students were able to achieve great success as professionals and became prominent figures in the Japanese American community. The Commemorative Fund's nisei are grateful for the time, effort, and compassion that the Student Relocation Council contributed to their higher education and to their future. Thus they sought to return the favor. Again they assume the role of Japanese American "ambassadors" spreading goodwill; however, this time they volunteer their time, effort, and financial support to help Southeast Asian students.

Most important, the National Student Relocation Commemorative Fund recognizes the need for interethnic support. After the Immigration Act of 1965 opened up immigration from Asian countries, the influx from Asia grew. This new group entering the United States differed greatly from those who came as laborers over four generations ago. However, the Commemorative Fund seeks to overcome such distinctions and work together with the youth of the new immigrants to give them hope for their future in America.

William M. Marutani, lawyer and former Common Pleas Court judge in Philadelphia, points out the significance of the Commemorative Fund's interethnic element: "I think it's one of the most beautiful charitable things around. The recipients are not people who have power. . . . It crosses ethnic lines. It's not Japanese Americans giving to Japanese Americans." Marutani received assistance from the Student Relocation Council after his education at the University of Washington was interrupted by the war. With the Council's help, he was able to finish his degree at Dakota Wesleyan University in Mitchell, South Dakota.[29]

In the spirit of *on-gaeshi*, the legacy of the National Japanese American Student Relocation Council continues. As the Southeast Asian award recipients have shown in their scholastic promise and their vision of the future, the tradition of helping others fulfill dreams of educational achievement will persevere. The Nisei Student Relocation Commemorative Fund exhibits a true commitment to pan-Asian unity and support.

NOTES

Preface

1. Frank Chin, Jeffery Paul Chan, Lawson Fusao Inada, and Shawn Wong, eds., *Aiiieeeee! An Anthology of Asian-American Writers* (Garden City, N.Y.: Anchor Press, 1975), pp. 8–9.

2. Carol Green Wilson, *Chinatown Quest: The Life Adventures of Donaldina Cameron* (Stanford: Stanford University Press, 1931); and Mildred Crowl Martin, *Chinatown's Angry Angel: The Story of Donaldina Cameron* (Palo Alto, Calif.: Pacific Books, 1977). Cf. Laurene Wu McClain, "Donaldina Cameron: A Reappraisal," *Pacific Historian* 27, no. 3 (Fall 1983): 25–35; and Peggy Pascoe, *Relations of Rescue: The Search for Female Moral Authority in the American West, 1874–1939* (New York: Oxford University Press, 1990).

3. "Success Story: Outwhiting the Whites," *Newsweek*, June 21, 1971, pp. 24–25.

4. Brian Niiya, ed., *Japanese American History: An A-to-Z Reference from 1868 to the Present* (New York: Facts on File, 1993), pp. 182–84, 184–85.

5. For example, see Gary Y. Okihiro, *Cane Fires: The Anti-Japanese Movement in Hawaii, 1865–1945* (Philadelphia: Temple University Press, 1991), pp. 129–62; and Sucheng Chan, "Race, Ethnic Culture, and Gender in the Construction of Identities among Second-Generation Chinese Americans, 1880s to 1930s," in *Claiming America: Constructing Chinese American Identities During the Exclusion Era*, ed. K. Scott Wong and Sucheng Chan (Philadelphia: Temple University Press, 1998), pp. 127–64. Cf. Eileen H. Tamura, *Americanization, Acculturation, and Ethnic Identity: The Nisei Generation in Hawaii* (Urbana: University of Illinois Press, 1994).

6. Quoted in Richard Drinnon, *Keeper of Concentration Camps: Dillon S. Myer and American Racism* (Berkeley: University of California Press, 1987), p. 50. For Myer's own account, see Dillon S. Myer, *Uprooted Americans: The Japanese Americans and the War Relocation Authority During World War II* (Tucson: University of Arizona Press, 1971).

7. For an account of the federal government's interventions in the lives of both American Indians and Japanese Americans, see Drinnon, *Keeper of Concentration Camps.*

8. Gary Y. Okihiro, *Teaching Asian American History* (Washington, D.C.: American Historical Association, 1997), pp. 31–57.

9. Thomas James, *Exile Within: The Schooling of Japanese Americans, 1942–1945* (Cambridge: Harvard University Press, 1987).

10. Robert W. O'Brien, *The College Nisei* (Palo Alto, Calif.: Pacific Books, 1949).

11. Thomas R. Bodine to author, December 5, 1997.

Chapter 1   An Uneventful Life

1. Roy Nakata, "The Story of My Life," in Alice Sinclair Dodge Collection, Hoover Institution, Stanford University, box 1, file "Correspondence 1942–1946."

2. Alice Sinclair Dodge to E. F. Bosworth, February 8, 1943, in Dodge Collection, box 1, file "Correspondence 1942–1946."

3. Roy Nakata to Alice Sinclair Dodge, July 30, 1942, in Dodge Collection, box 1, file "Correspondence 1942–1946."

4. Roy Nakata to Alice Sinclair Dodge, June 4, 1942, in Dodge Collection, box 1, file "Correspondence 1942–1946."

5. Roy Nakata to Alice Sinclair Dodge, December 6, 1942, in Dodge Collection, box 1, file "Correspondence 1942–1946."

6. See Richard Polenberg, "The Good War? A Reappraisal of How World War II Affected American Society," *Virginia Magazine of History and Biography* 100, no. 3 (July 1992): 295–322.

7. See also "Nisei: Disguised Blessing," *Newsweek*, December 29, 1958, p. 23; and William Petersen, *Japanese Americans: Oppression and Success* (New York: Random House, 1971), pp. 3–5.

8. For a review of the stereotype's evolution, see Keith Osajima, "Asian Americans as the Model Minority: An Analysis of the Popular Press Image in the 1960s and 1980s," in *Reflections on Shattered Windows: Promises and Prospects for Asian American Studies,* ed. Gary Y. Okihiro et al. (Pullman: Washington State University Press, 1988), pp. 165–74. For a critique, see Ronald Takaki, *Strangers from a Different Shore: A History of Asian Americans* (Boston: Little, Brown, 1989), pp. 474–84; and Sucheng Chan, *Asian Americans: An Interpretive History* (Boston: Twayne, 1991), pp. 167–81. For an analysis of the "model minority" and "yellow peril" stereotypes, see Gary Y. Okihiro, *Margins and Mainstreams: Asians in American History and Culture* (Seattle: University of Washington Press, 1994), pp. 118–47.

9. *The Log of Christopher Columbus,* trans. Robert H. Fuson (Camden, Maine: International Marine Publishing, 1987), p. 51.

10. Henry Nash Smith, *Virgin Land: The American West as Symbol and Myth* (Cambridge: Harvard University Press, 1950), pp. 17, 19, 21.

11. Cited in Ronald Takaki, *Pau Hana: Plantation Life and Labor in Hawaii, 1835–1920* (Honolulu: University of Hawaii Press, 1983), pp. 23, 24.

12. Eileen Sunada Sarasohn, ed., *The Issei: Portrait of a Pioneer* (Palo Alto: Pacific Books, 1983), pp. 49–50, 51, 55–56.

13. Ibid., pp. 76–78.

14. Timothy J. Lukes and Gary Y. Okihiro, *Japanese Legacy: Farming and Community Life in California's Santa Clara Valley* (Cupertino: California History Center, 1985), pp. 24–25.

15. Quoted in Yuji Ichioka, *The Issei: The World of the First Generation Japanese Immigrants, 1885–1924* (New York: Free Press, 1988), p. 83.

16. Sarasohn, *Issei*, pp. 83–84.

17. Kazuo Ito, *Issei: A History of Japanese Immigrants in North America*, trans. Shinichiro Nakamura and Jean S. Gerard (Seattle: Japanese Community Service, 1973), pp. 249–50.

18. Sarasohn, *Issei*, pp. 63, 64, 68.

19. Quoted in Roger Daniels, *Concentration Camps: North America, Japanese in the United States and Canada During World War II* (Malabar, Fla.: Robert E. Krieger Publishing, 1981), p. 23.

20. Essay in Louis Adamic, *From Many Lands* (New York: Harper & Brothers, 1939), pp. 221–22, 233, 234.

21. Cited in Thomas James, *Exile Within: The Schooling of Japanese Americans, 1942–1945* (Cambridge: Harvard University Press, 1987), p. 21.

22. Gary Y. Okihiro, *Cane Fires: The Anti-Japanese Movement in Hawaii, 1865–1945* (Philadelphia: Temple University Press, 1991), pp. 78, 79, 97, 113.

23. Ibid., pp. 116, 117.

24. Ibid., pp. 118, 124–25, 128.

25. Ibid., pp. 173–75.

26. Bob Kumamoto, "The Search for Spies: American Counterintelligence and the Japanese American Community, 1931–1942," *Amerasia Journal* 6, no. 2 (1979): 45–75.

27. John Tateishi, *And Justice for All: An Oral History of the Japanese American Detention Camps* (New York: Random House, 1984), p. 5.

28. Lothrop Stoddard, *The Rising Tide of Color Against White World-Supremacy* (New York: Charles Scribner's Sons, 1920).

29. Tateishi, *And Justice for All*, p. 5.

30. Quoted in Andrew W. Lind, *Hawaii's Japanese: An Experiment in Democracy* (Princeton: Princeton University Press, 1946), p. 102.

31. Kiyo Hirano, *Enemy Alien* (San Francisco: JAM Publications, 1983), p. 3.

32. Cited in Morton Grodzins, *Americans Betrayed: Politics and the Japanese Evacuation* (Chicago: University of Chicago Press, 1949), p. 380. For surveys of press coverage during this period, see Gary Y. Okihiro and Julie Sly, "The Press, Japanese Americans, and the Concentrations Camps," *Phylon* 44, no.1 (March 1983): 66–83; and Grodzins, *Americans Betrayed*, pp. 377–99.

33. Toru Matsumoto, *Beyond Prejudice: A Story of the Church and Japanese Americans* (New York: Friendship Press, 1946), p. 10.

34. Hirano, *Enemy Alien*, pp. 5–6.

35. Quoted in Daniels, *Concentration Camps*, pp. 55–56.

36. Roger Daniels, *The Decision to Relocate the Japanese Americans* (Philadelphia: J. B. Lippincott, 1975), pp. 34–35.

37. Take Uchida, "An Issei Internee's Experiences," in *Japanese Americans: From Relocation to Redress,* rev. ed., ed. Roger Daniels, Sandra C. Taylor, and Harry H. L. Kitano (Seattle: University of Washington Press, 1991), p. 31.

38. Daisuke Kitagawa, *Issei and Nisei: The Internment Years* (New York: Seabury Press, 1967), p. 41.

39. Matsumoto, *Beyond Prejudice,* pp. 10–12.

40. Okihiro, *Cane Fires,* p. 228.

41. Grodzins, *Americans Betrayed,* pp. 27–28.

42. Daniels, *Concentration Camps,* p. 65.

43. Audrie Girdner and Anne Loftis, *The Great Betrayal: The Evacuation of the Japanese-Americans During World War II* (London: Macmillan, 1969), p. 112.

44. Bill Hosokawa, *Nisei: The Quiet Americans* (New York: William Morrow, 1969), p. 310.

45. Girdner and Loftis, *Great Betrayal,* pp. 112–13.

46. Ibid., p. 112.

47. Ibid., p. 113.

Chapter 2   Toward a Better Society

1. "Nisei Students Speak for Themselves: A Symposium," *Junior College Journal* 14, no. 6 (February 1944): 243–44.

2. Hosokawa, *Nisei,* p. 308.

3. Sarasohn, *Issei,* p. 166.

4. Robert W. O'Brien, *The College Nisei* (Palo Alto: Pacific Books, 1949), p. 62.

5. W. C. Coffey to Robert M. Hutchins, March 18, 1942, President's Papers, University Archives, University of Minnesota, Minneapolis. I am grateful to Lois G. Hendrickson, assistant archivist, for locating and copying materials from this collection.

6. A. C. Willard to W. C. Coffey, March 20, 1942, President's Papers, Minnesota.

7. Deane W. Malott to W. C. Coffey, March 21, 1942. Despite Malott's desire, the University of Kansas's board, after having consulted with the F B I, decided to close the state's schools to Japanese Americans. Malott to Coffey, April 7, 1942.

8. Board of Regents Minutes, January 16, 1942, to December 17, 1943, Archives, University of Colorado, Boulder. I am grateful to Marty Covey, University Libraries, University of Colorado, for her assistance in locating and copying these minutes.

9. Joseph W. Conard to Uncle Henry and Aunt Laetitia, May 2, 1942, Records of the National Japanese American Student Relocation Council,

1942–1946, Hoover Institution Archives, Stanford University (hereafter NJASRC), box 6, file "Joseph Conard."

10. Henry Conard to Joseph W. Conard, May 9, 1942, ibid.

11. C. A. Dykstra to W. C. Coffey, April 2, 1942, President's Papers, Minnesota.

12. W. C. Coffey to Fred J. Kelly, April 8, 1942, President's Papers, Minnesota.

13. Fred J. Kelly to W. C. Coffey, April 15, 1942, President's Papers, Minnesota.

14. George F. Zook to W. C. Coffey, April 29, 1942, President's Papers, Minnesota.

15. Apparently, Eisenhower had asked Zook to head the committee, but he had declined. Guy Stanton Ford to Malcolm M. Willey, June 19, 1942, President's Papers, Minnesota.

16. M. S. Eisenhower to C. E. Pickett, May 5, 1942, NJASRC, box 110, file "Property of Dr. Robbin[s] W. Barstow" (hereafter Barstow file).

17. Ibid.

18. Clarence E. Pickett to Robbins W. Barstow, May 9, 1942, NJASRC, box 110, Barstow file.

19. Robbins W. Barstow to Joseph Conard, July 16, 1942, NJASRC, box 38, file "Dr. Barstow—Philadelphia Office."

20. Eisenhower to Pickett, May 5, 1942.

21. Yukio Nakayama to Professor Ellwood, May 20, 1942, NJASRC, box 110, Barstow file.

22. Pickett to Barstow, May 9, 1942.

23. John J. McCloy to Clarence E. Pickett, May 21, 1942, NJASRC, box 110, Barstow file.

24. Apparently the JACL in May 1942 had conducted a survey of colleges and universities regarding their receptivity to nisei students, but by August they had left the work of student relocation. NJASRC, box 10, file "JACL."

25. "Digest of Points Presented By Those Attending the Conference Called in Chicago for the Consideration of the Problems Connected with Relocation of the American-Born Japanese Students Who Have Been Evacuated from Pacific Coast Colleges and Universities," May 29, 1942, NJASRC, box 110, Barstow file.

26. Ibid.

27. Ibid.

28. For a synopsis of this process of student evaluation, see Margaret Cosgrave, "Relocation of American-Japanese Students," *Journal of the American Association of Collegiate Registrars,* April 1943, pp. 221–26.

29. "Procedure for Analysis of Student Qualifications," n.d. [stamped August 10, 1942], NJASRC, box 35, file "Pacific Coast Branch, Japanese Situation."

30. "Procedure Concerning Community Acceptance," July 24, 1942, NJASRC, box 35, file "Pacific Coast Branch, Japanese Situation."

31. National Student Relocation Council to WCCA Regulatory Section, July 30, 1942, NJASRC, box 35, file "Pacific Coast Branch, Japanese Situation."

32. Barstow to Conard, July 16, 1942.

33. John H. Provinse to Robbins W. Barstow, June 24, 1942, NJASRC, box 38, file "Dr. Barstow—Philadelphia."

34. Progress Report, October 1, 1942, NJASRC, box 36, file "Pacific Coast Branch . . . 1942"; and the pamphlet *From Camp to College: The Story of Japanese American Student Relocation* (Philadelphia: National Japanese American Student Relocation Council, n.d.). Cf. Brief Report of Progress, December 24, 1942, NJASRC, box 35, file "Pacific Coast Branch, Japanese Situation . . . , November and December 1942," that states that 800 had been accepted and 334 attended college that fall. *From Camp to College* was written by Thomas R. Bodine; correspondence Bodine to Okihiro, December 5, 1997.

35. Brief Report of Progress, December 24, 1942.

36. Personnel and Finances, December 15, 1942, NJASRC, box 38, file "West Coast Reports on . . . Salaries."

37. Margaret Cosgrave Sowers, oral history interview, December 11, 1993.

38. Joseph Conard to Director of Admissions, Drake University, August 26, 1942, NJASRC, box 110, file "West Coast, Letters to Colleges."

39. Joseph Conard to Willis R. Jones, August 28, 1942, NJASRC, box 110, folder "West Coast, Letters to Colleges."

40. Edwin C. Morgenroth to Robbins W. Barstow, July 31, 1942, NJASRC, box 1, file "Advisory Committee for Evacuees, Chicago."

41. Advisory Committee on Planning for Evacuees in Chicago, Organization Meeting, July 28, 1942, NJASRC, box 1, file "Advisory Committee for Evacuees, Chicago."

42. Morgenroth to Barstow, July 31, 1942.

43. Report as of September 30, 1942, NJASRC, box 1, file "Advisory Committee for Evacuees, Chicago."

44. Margaret T. Morewood with the assistance of Florence Scott, "A Review of the First 400 Japanese-American Students To Be Relocated by the National Student Relocation Council," San Francisco, February 1943, NJASRC, box 91, file "Report—A Review of the First 400. . . ."

Chapter 3   Exemplars

1. Morewood and Scott, "A Review of the First 400 Japanese-American Students."

2. Series of letters included in Thomas R. Bodine Papers, Hoover Institution, Stanford University, box 7, file 6 "The Story of *One* Student's Relocation, March 1942/May 1943."

3. Letters from Walter Funabiki dated September 30, October 3, November 3, November 17, and December 14, 1942; January 4, February 24, March

28, April 9, April 18, July 30, August 15, and September 27, 1943; Bodine Papers, box 7, file 7.

4. Letters from Wiley Higuchi dated August 25, 1942; May 3, June 27, July 24, August 1, December 1, and December 16, 1943; January 3, January 7, April 1, July 19, and August 10, 1944; NJASRC, box 115, file "Wiley Higuchi."

5. Quoted in Valerie Matsumoto, "Japanese American Women During World War II," in *Unequal Sisters: A Multicultural Reader in U.S. Women's History*, ed. Ellen Carol DuBois and Vicki L. Ruiz (New York: Routledge, 1990), p. 380.

6. Letter dated August 28, 1942, Bodine Papers, box 7, file 7.

7. Letter dated September 10, 1942, Bodine Papers, box 7, file 7.

8. Jeanne Mori to Tom Bodine, July 5, 1942, and Mabel Sugiyama to Danny Wilcher, February 13, 1943, both in Bodine Papers, box 8, file 8.2.

9. Cited in Leslie A. Ito, "Loyalty and Learning: Nisei Women and the Student Relocation" (B.A. honors thesis, Mount Holyoke College, 1996), pp. 23–26.

10. Leslie Ito has suggested a class dimension to this issei desire to educate both their male and female children. Ibid., pp. 21–22.

11. Esther Torii Suzuki, "Memoirs," in *Reflections: Memoirs of Japanese American Women in Minnesota*, ed. John Nobuya Tsuchida (Covina, Calif.: Pacific Asia Press, 1994), pp. 89–126.

12. Nao Takasugi to Akio Konoshima, February 9, 1946, NJASRC, box 115, file "Akio Konoshima."

13. M. Joan Smith, "Backgrounds, Problems and Significant Reactions of Re-located Japanese American Students" (Ed.D. dissertation, Syracuse University, 1949), p. 49.

14. Woodruff J. Emlen to Nell V. Beeby, August 16, 1943, NJASRC, box 1, file A, vol. 2.

15. Helen W. Munson to W. J. Emlen, August 27, 1943, NJASRC, box 1, file A, vol. 2.

16. Woodruff J. Emlen to Helen W. Munson, August 31, 1943; Munson to Emlen, September 3, 1943; Emlen to Munson, September 8, 1943; Munson to Emlen, September 10, 1043; and Emlen to *American Journal of Nursing*, September 17, 1943, NJASRC, box 1, file A, vol. 2.

17. "The Problem of Student Nurses of Japanese Ancestry," *American Journal of Nursing* 43, no. 10 (October 1943): 895–96.

18. Smith, "Backgrounds, Problems and Significant Reactions," pp. 108–10.

19. Constance Murayama to Trudy King, July 8, 1943, Bodine Papers, box 7, file 16.

20. Haruko Morita to Trudy King, September 29, 1943, Bodine Papers, box 7, file 16.

21. Kazuko Nakamura to Trudy King, November 13, 1943, Bodine Papers, box 7, file 17.

22. Mary Ogi, October 7, 1942, Bodine Papers, box 7, file 8; and Ruth Hide Dohi, November 25, 1942, Bodine Papers, box 7, file 9.

23. Cited in Girdner and Loftis, *Great Betrayal,* p. 337.

24. Quoted in O'Brien, *College Nisei,* p. 87.

25. From clippings in Bodine Papers, box 5, file 5.1.

26. Albert K. Mineta, November 7, 1942; and Dohi, November 25, 1942, Bodine Papers, box 7, file 9.

27. O'Brien, *College Nisei,* pp. 88–89.

28. Kiyo Sato, March 2, 1943, Bodine Papers, box 7, file 12.

Chapter 4   Yearbook Portraits

1. Naomi Iwasaki, statement submitted with her application for admission form to Park College. I am grateful to Harold F. Smith, archivist, Park College, Parkville, Missouri, for finding and copying this material for me.

2. Barnett Turk, "A Land-Locked World Away," *Alumni Voice* (University of Missouri, Kansas City), Summer 1987, p. 3. Marilyn Burlingame, archives assistant, University of Missouri, Kansas City, searched for and copied these materials for me, for which I am grateful.

3. Ibid., pp. 3, 4.

4. William W. Hall, Jr., *The Small College Talks Back: An Intimate Appraisal* (New York: Richard R. Smith, 1951), pp. 63–67. I gratefully acknowledge the help provided by Sylvia Tag, archivist at Albertson College of Idaho, who called my attention to this work.

5. *The Trail,* 1942, 1943, 1944, College of Idaho, Caldwell, Idaho. Archivist Sylvia Tag located and photocopied this information for me.

6. LeRoy E. Cowles, *University of Utah and World War II* (Salt Lake City: Deseret News Press, 1949), pp. 37, 39–40; and LeRoy E. Cowles to L. P. Sieg, March 21, 1942, Archives, University of Utah, Salt Lake City. I am indebted to Kirk H. Baddley, archivist, and Walter Jones, head of the Western Americana Division of the Special Collections Department, University Libraries, University of Utah, Salt Lake City, for finding and sending me this information.

7. Andrea Wood Cranford, "Not an Enemy," in *A Commemorative Album,* University of Nebraska–Lincoln Nisei Reunion, November 4–5, 1994, pp. 4, 5, 6, 23, 38. I am grateful to Andrea Cranford, director of communications and editor of the *Nebraska,* University of Nebraska–Lincoln, for sending me this booklet and information on Nebraska's nisei students.

8. Guy Montag, "The Grinnell Nisei," manuscript, Grinnell College, May 17, 1984, p. 3. I am grateful to Mary V. Grey, acting assistant college archivist, Grinnell College, for locating Montag's paper, written for a history class and filed in the college archives, and to Guy Montag for releasing his paper to me for use in this volume.

9. Ibid., pp. 2, 3–4, 6.

10. H. Quintus Sakai to Guy R. Montag, April 23, 1984, quoted ibid., pp. 7, 8.

11. Interview with Barbara Takahashi Yamaguchi, May 2, 1984, ibid., notes.

12. Sakai to Montag, April 23, 1984, ibid., notes.

13. Questionnaires filled out by Ruth Berglund Ryder and Georgianna Smith (Hochstein), ibid., notes.

14. *Zenith,* 1944, Simpson College, Indianola, Iowa, p. 73. I am grateful to Cynthia M. Dyer, director of library service, Dunn Library, Simpson College, for locating and photocopying this material.

15. I am grateful to Barry Bunch, assistant archivist, University Archives, Kenneth Spencer Research Library, University of Kansas, Lawrence, Kansas, for finding this information for me.

16. *Berea Citizen,* November 25, 1943.

17. *Berea Citizen,* December 2, 1943.

18. Shannon H. Wilson, college archivist, Hutchins Library, Berea College, Berea, Kentucky, found and sent me this information, for which I am grateful.

19. I thank Patricia J. Albright, archives librarian, Mount Holyoke College Archives, South Hadley, Massachusetts, for sending me this information.

20. *Oberlin Alumni Magazine,* Fall 1995, p. 13. I thank Christopher Densmore, associate archivist, University at Buffalo, New York, for sending me this information.

21. Lynn Ruth Miller, "Farewell to Heart Mountain: Welcome to Toledo," *The Blade Sunday Magazine,* August 8, 1976, p. 5. Barbara Floyd, university archivist, University of Toledo, Toledo, Ohio, collected this information, for which I am thankful.

22. I am indebted to Paul T. Hayashi, Frederick Hayashi's son, for releasing his father's Perkins files to me for this book. Barbara E. Leone, registrar, Perkins School for the Blind, Watertown, Massachusetts, located and copied for me Hayashi's files, for which I am grateful.

23. Grace C. Hamman to Gabriel Farrell, October 10, 1938, Records, Perkins School for the Blind, Watertown, Massachusetts.

24. J. P. Buller to Gabriel Farrell, January 31, 1939, Records, Perkins.

25. Grace C. Hamman to Gabriel Farrell, April 26, 1939, Records, Perkins.

26. Asao Hayashi, September 4, 1939, Records, Perkins.

27. Anna G. Fish to Asao Hayashi, September 13, 1939, Records, Perkins.

28. Frederick Hayashi, Personnel Department, September 25, 1939; and Francis M. Andrews to Asao Hayashi, January 31, 1940, Records, Perkins.

29. Frederick Hayashi, Summary, Records, Perkins.

30. See, for example, Peter Irons, *Justice At War* (New York: Oxford University Press, 1983); *Personal Justice Denied,* Report of the Commission on Wartime Relocation and Internment of Civilians (Washington, D.C.: Government Printing Office, 1982); and Roger Daniels, *Prisoners Without Trial: Japanese Americans in World War II* (New York: Hill and Wang, 1993).

31. Quoted in Daniels, *Concentration Camps,* p. 65.

32. W. C. Coffey to Henry L. Stimson, September 30, 1942, University Archives, University of Minnesota, Minneapolis. I am grateful to Penelope Krosch, archivist and head, and Lois G. Hendrickson, assistant archivist, University of Minnesota, Minneapolis, for finding and sending me these materials.

33. John J. McCloy to W. C. Coffey, October 6, 1942; John H. Provinse to Coffey, October 9, 1942 (WRA response); and James Forrestal to Coffey, October 12, 1942, Archives, University of Minnesota.

34. Malcolm M. Willey to W. C. Coffey, October 15, 1942, Archives, University of Minnesota.

35. Malcolm M. Willey to John H. Provinse, October 22, 1942; Howard K. Beale to W. C. Coffey, November 22, 1942; Howard K. Beale to Malcolm M. Willey, November 22, 1942; Malcolm M. Willey to Howard K. Beale, December 1, 1942; and Howard K. Beale to Malcolm M. Willey, December 9, 1942, Archives, University of Minnesota.

36. W. C. Coffey to James Forrestal, June 3, 1943; Forrestal to Coffey, June 14, 1943, Archives, University of Minnesota.

37. W. C. Coffey to Malcolm M. Willey, June 19, 1943; Malcolm M. Willey to Commanding General, Seventh Service Command, November 4, 1943, Archives, University of Minnesota.

38. W. C. Coffey to T. E. Pettengill, December 1, 1943, Archives, University of Minnesota.

39. Rex A. Ramsay to Malcolm M. Willey, April 11, 1944, Archives, University of Minnesota.

40. *University of Nevada Sagebrush,* April 3 and 17, 1942; and Minutes of the Board of Regents, May 9, 1942, University Archives, University of Nevada, Reno. I am grateful to Karen Gash, archivist, University Library, University of Nevada, Reno, for finding and copying this material for me.

41. Minutes of the Board of Regents, May 9, 1942, October 2, 1943, and September 22, 1945, University Archives, University of Nevada; and Karen Gash to Gary Y. Okihiro, August 4, 1995.

42. *Blue Mantle,* 1944; *Saint Mary's Static,* November 1943, February 1944, April 1944, March 1946, April 1946, and May 1946; *Chimes* 54, no. 3 (Spring 1945). I am grateful to Sister M. Rosaleen Dunleavy, CSG, Cushwa-Leighton Library, Saint Mary's College, Notre Dame, Indiana, for locating and photocopying this information.

43. I gratefully acknowledge the work of Mel Doering, archivist, Valparaiso University, Valparaiso, Indiana, for finding and reporting this information to me.

44. Maxine Kreutziger, of the Kansas East Commission on Archives and History, Baker University, sent me this information, for which I am grateful.

45. I am grateful to Carole Prietto, university archivist, Olin Library, Washington University, St. Louis, for collecting this material for me.

46. Bonnie Knauss, reference/special collections librarian, Curry Library,

William Jewell College, Liberty, Missouri, located and copied this information, for which I am grateful.

47. Jean A. Schoenthaler, library director and archivist, Drew University, Madison, New Jersey, kindly copied this information for me.

48. Jane Lowenthal, archivist, Barnard College, New York City, gathered this information for me, for which I am grateful.

49. I thank Pat Patton, University Archives, Kansas State University, Manhattan, Kansas, for locating and sending me this information.

50. Karen K. Oswalt, archivist, Morrison Kenyon Library, Asbury College, Wilmore, Kentucky, sent me this information, for which I am grateful.

51. I thank Jerome A. Fallon, archivist and historian, Hillsdale College, Hillsdale, Michigan, for finding and copying these materials for me.

52. *Kalamazoo College Quarterly*, Fall/Winter 1992–93, pp. 4–6. Carol P. Smith and Liz Smith, college archivist, sent me this information, for which I am thankful.

53. I am grateful to Bertha L. Ihnat, archives assistant, University Archives, Ohio State University, Columbus, Ohio, for clipping this information from the university directory and yearbook, *Makio*.

54. *The Wellesley News*, March 14, 1990, pp. 12–13. I am grateful to Wilma R. Slaight, archivist, Margaret Clapp Library, Wellesley College, Wellesley, Massachusetts, for sending me this information.

55. Jack Robson, director of library and media services, Nebraska Wesleyan University, Lincoln, Nebraska, supplied me this information taken from yearbooks and newspaper clippings. I am grateful to him for having been "carried away with this little project," as he put it.

56. I am grateful to Dorothy Huss, assistant librarian, Ella McIntire Library, Huron University, Sioux Falls, South Dakota, for clipping and sending me this information.

Chapter 5   A Thousand Cranes

1. John W. Nason to the Presidents of Colleges, Universities and Professional Schools, November 26, 1942, Archives, Library Learning Center, University of Wisconsin–Stout, Menomonie, Wisconsin. I am grateful to Kevin Thorie, university archivist, for finding and copying this material for me.

2. *Cornell Report* 14, no. 3 (Spring/Summer 1991). I thank Roberta Ringold, college archivist, Cornell College, Mount Vernon, Iowa, for sending me this information.

3. Masako Amemiya MacFarlane, oral history interview, December 15, 1995.

4. I am grateful to Jean A. Schoenthaler, library director and university archivist, Drew University, Madison, New Jersey, for providing me with this information.

5. Albert K. Mineta, oral history interview, December 15, 1995.

6. Louise Seki Hoare, oral history interview, November 3, 1995.

7. Mary Otani, oral history interview, December 14, 1995.

8. These letters to Betty Udall are in the possession of Mary Otani.

9. I am grateful to Mary Otani for sharing with me copies of her letters to her family.

10. Agnes Kawate, oral history interview, November 3, 1995.

11. Alice Matsumoto, oral history interview, April 12, 1996; and Alice Abe Matsumoto, "Memoirs," in *Reflections*, ed. Tsuchida, pp. 371–89.

12. Yoshio Matsumoto, oral history interview, April 12, 1996.

13. George Matsumoto, oral history interview, December 14, 1995.

14. Min Yoshida, oral history interview, April 13, 1996.

15. Maye Mitsuye Oye Uemura, "Memoirs," in *Reflections*, ed. Tsuchida, p. 365.

16. Maye Uemura, oral history interview, April 12, 1996.

17. Uemura, "Memoirs," pp. 365–66.

18. June Kawamura, oral history interview, November 4, 1995.

19. I thank Mark Wiesenberg, communication coordinator, David Eccles School of Business, University of Utah, Salt Lake City, Utah, for sending me these materials.

Chapter 6   Antiracism

1. Report of the Field Director to the National Japanese American Student Relocation Council, September 29, 1943, NJASRC, box 4, file "Thomas R. Bodine, Reports and Correspondence."

2. Marjorie Hyer to Bob O'Brien, October 28, 1942, NJASRC, box 2, file "American Friends Service Committee, General Correspondence."

3. Joe Alter letter, April 19, 1942; Abraham Akaka to Joseph Conard, May 9, 1942; and Conard to Akaka, May 16, 1942, all in NJASRC, box 1, file A "General Correspondence."

4. *From Camp to College.*

5. Rei Sakaizawa to E. A. Corey, July 7, 1943, NJASRC, box 42, No Records File.

6. "Final Composite Report of the Returnee Nisei College Leaders, Summer of 1944," NJASRC, box 45, file "Final Composite Report. . . ."

7. Marion Konishi to Tom Bodine, October 2, 1944; Philip Nagao to Tom Bodine, October 3, 1944, NJASRC, box 44, file "1944 Returnee Project Final Report."

8. Haruo Ishimaru, "Final Report Covering August 24th Through September 18, 1944," September 18, 1944, NJASRC, box 44, file "1944 Returnee Project Final Report."

9. "Final Composite Report . . . Summer of 1944," NJASRC, box 45, file "Final Composite Report. . . ."

10. Frank T. Inouye to John W. Nason, August 16, 1944; Nason to Inouye, August 24, 1944, NJASRC, box 13, file "John W. Nason, 1944."

11. "Final Composite Report—Student Returnee Project, Summer 1945," NJASRC, box 44, file "TRB's Returnee Report."

12. Esther Takei to Nao Takasugi, June 5, 1945, NJASRC, box 43, file "Esther Takei."

13. Eugene Ueki to Nao Takasugi, August 18, 1945, NJASRC, box 45, file "Minidoka, 1945 Returnee Project."

14. Samuel Ishikawa to Nao Takasugi and Mrs. Wilkerson, August 6, 1945, NJASRC, box 45, file "Manzanar, 1945 Returnee Project."

15. Thomas R. Bodine, oral history interview, May 18, 1994.

16. *From Camp to College.*

17. *Personal Justice Denied,* pp. 2–3.

18. Dillon S. Myer, *Uprooted Americans: The Japanese Americans and the War Relocation Authority During World War II* (Tucson: University of Arizona Press, 1971), p. 286.

19. Richard Drinnon, *Keeper of Concentration Camps: Dillon S. Myer and American Racism* (Berkeley: University of California Press, 1987), pp. 50, 59.

20. Mary Otani, oral history interview, December 14, 1995.

21. Mas Yamada, March 2, 1943, Bodine Papers, Hoover, box 7, file 12.

22. Pickett to Barstow, May 9, 1942; and Barstow to Conard, July 16, 1942.

23. John W. Nason to Howard K. Beale, November 7, 1942, NJASRC, box 35, file "Branch, Pacific Coast, Japanese Situation (corres. w/San Francisco)."

24. Barstow to Conard, July 17, 1942.

25. Quoted in Daniels, *Concentration Camps,* p. 91.

26. Quoted in Hosokawa, *Nisei,* pp. 346, 347.

27. John W. Nason, oral history interview, June 9, 1994.

28. Barbara Haddad Ryan, "From Camps to Campus," *Swarthmore College Bulletin,* February 1993, p. 22.

29. John W. Nason, oral history interview, June 9, 1994; and Ryan, "From Camps to Campus," p. 24.

30. Ann Graybill Cook, oral history interview, June 10, 1994.

31. Betty Emlen and Woodruff J. Emlen, oral history interview, June 9, 1994.

32. Thomas R. Bodine, oral history interview, May 18, 1994.

33. Thomas R. Bodine to Friends of Germantown Meeting, May 8, 1943, Bodine Papers, Hoover, box 1, file 1.1.

34. Kay Yamashita, oral history interview, April 6, 1994.

35. Toru Matsumoto to Betty Emlen, October 11, 1944, NJASRC, box 40, file "General H."

36. Kay Yamashita to Vickie Hata, October 21, 1944, NJASRC, box 40, file "General H."

37. Vickie Hata to Kay Yamashita, November 9, 1944, NJASRC, box 40, file "General H."

38. Kay Yamashita to Vickie Hata, November 17, 1944, NJASRC, box 40, file "General H."

39. Helen Aihara to "Friends," September 4, 1943, NJASRC, box 40, file "General A."

40. *From Camp to College.* Cf. O'Brien, *College Nisei,* p. 67.

41. O'Brien, *College Nisei,* p. 67.

42. Daniels, *Concentration Camps,* p. 56.

43. Kay Yamashita, "A Short History of the National Japanese American Student Relocation Council and the Nisei Student Relocation Commemorative Fund," typescript, oral history folder.

44. Herbert Aptheker, *Anti-Racism in U.S. History: The First Two Hundred Years* (Westport, Conn.: Praeger, 1993), p. xiii.

45. Lafayette Noda to E. C. Adams, July 19, 1943, Bodine Papers, Hoover, box 7, file 16.

46. Kiyo Ogawa to Betty Emlen, May 8, 1945, NJASRC, box 113, file "Kiyo Ogawa."

Afterword

1. Chiyo Moriuchi, speech, NSRC Awards Ceremony, New York City, June 21, 1996.

2. Nobu Hibino, oral history interview with Gary Okihiro, May 18, 1994.

3. Moriuchi, speech.

4. Lafayette Noda, oral history interview with Gary Okihiro, May 18, 1994.

5. See Bill Hosokawa, "A Good Man, A Good Cause," *Pacific Citizen,* December 4–11, 1992; and J. K. Yamamoto, "Members of the Japanese American Student Relocation Council Honored," *Hokubei Mainichi,* April 22, 1995.

6. Nobu Hibino to Leslie Ito, July 25, 1996.

7. Noda, interview.

8. Bill Marutani, "AFSC Remembered," *Pacific Citizen,* June 18, 1982.

9. Moriuchi, speech.

10. Testimony Before the California Legislature Joint Committee on Refugee Resettlement and Immigration, May 6, 1983.

11. Moriuchi, speech.

12. Lydia Villalva, "12 Southeast Asian Students Awarded Scholarships," *St. Paul Pioneer Press Dispatch,* May 10, 1987, p. 1B.

13. Sucheng Chan, *Asian Americans: An Interpretive History* (Boston: Twayne, 1991), pp. 154–56.

14. Vung G. Thuy, "The Indochinese in America," in *The Education of Asian and Pacific Americans: Historical Perspectives and Prescriptions for the Future,* ed. Don T. Nakanishi and Marsha Hirano-Nakanishi. (Phoenix: Onyx Press, 1983), p. 106.

15. Nazli Kibria, *Family Tightrope: The Changing Lives of Vietnamese Americans* (Princeton: Princeton University Press, 1993), p. 85.

16. Kenji Ima and Ruben G. Rumbaut, "Southeast Asian Refugees in American Schools: A Comparison of Fluent-English-Proficient and Limited-

English-Proficient Students," in *The Asian American Educational Experience: A Source Book for Teachers and Students,* ed. Don T. Nakanishi and Tina Yamano Nishida (New York: Routledge, 1995), p. 182.

17. Chan, *Asian Americans,* p. 157.

18. Ibid., p. 161.

19. 1990 NSRC Fund Scholarship Winners, Philadelphia, Pennsylvania.

20. Leark Vath e-mail to Leslie Ito, May 19, 1997.

21. 1983 NSRC Fund Scholarship Winners, Berkeley, California.

22. Mayna Moua e-mail to Leslie Ito, May 19, 1997.

23. Kibria, *Family Tightrope,* p. 74.

24. 1993 NSRC Fund Scholarship Winners, Stockton, California.

25. 1992 NSRC Fund Scholarship Winners, New England.

26. 1983 NSRC Fund Scholarship Winners, Berkeley, California.

27. Dale Mezzacappa, "Survivors at the Head of the Class," *Philadelphia Inquirer,* June 14, 1990, p. 1A.

28. 1990 NSRC Fund Scholarship Winners, Philadelphia, Pennsylvania.

29. Murray Dublin, "Helped Long Ago, They Help Now," *Philadelphia Inquirer,* May 15, 1990, p. 1B.

BIBLIOGRAPHY

Documents

Archives, Morrison Kenyon Library, Asbury College, Wilmore, Kentucky.

Kansas East Commission on Archives and History, Baker University.

Archives, Barnard College, New York City.

Archives, Hutchins Library, Berea College, Berea, Kentucky.

Archives, University Libraries, University of Colorado, Boulder.

Archives, Cornell College, Mount Vernon, Iowa.

Archives, Drew University, Madison, New Jersey.

Archives, Hillsdale College, Hillsdale, Michigan.

Archives, Ella McIntire Library, Huron University, Sioux Falls, South Dakota.

Archives, College of Idaho, Caldwell, Idaho.

Archives, Kalamazoo College, Kalamazoo, Michigan.

University Archives, Kenneth Spencer Research Library, University of Kansas, Lawrence.

University Archives, Kansas State University, Manhattan, Kansas.

President's Papers, University Archives, University of Minnesota, Minneapolis.

Archives, University of Missouri–Kansas City.

Archives, Mount Holyoke College, South Hadley, Massachusetts.

Archives, University of Nebraska–Lincoln.

Library and Media Services, Nebraska Wesleyan University, Lincoln, Nebraska.

Archives, University Library, University of Nevada, Reno.

University Archives, Ohio State University, Columbus.

Archives, Park College, Parkville, Missouri.

Registrars' Records, Perkins School for the Blind, Watertown, Massachusetts.

Archives, Cushwa-Leighton Library, Saint Mary's College, Notre Dame, Indiana.

Archives, Simpson College, Indianola, Iowa.

Thomas R. Bodine Papers, Hoover Institution, Stanford University.

Alice Sinclair Dodge Collection, Hoover Institution, Stanford University.

Frank B. Duveneck Collection, Hoover Institution, Stanford University.

John W. Nason Papers, Hoover Institution, Stanford University.
Records of the National Japanese American Student Relocation Council, 1942–1946, Hoover Institution, Stanford University.
Grace Nichols Pearson Papers, Hoover Institution, Stanford University.
Margaret Cosgrave Sowers Papers, Hoover Institution, Stanford University.
Archives, University of Toledo, Toledo, Ohio.
Archives, University Libraries, University of Utah, Salt Lake City.
Archives, Valparaiso University, Valparaiso, Indiana.
Archives, Olin Library, Washington University, St. Louis, Missouri.
Archives, Margaret Clapp Library, Wellesley College, Wellesley, Massachusetts.
Special Collections, Curry Library, William Jewell College, Liberty, Missouri.
Archives, Library Learning Center, University of Wisconsin–Stout, Menomonie.

Oral Histories

Thomas R. Bodine, May 18, 1994, Bloomfield, Connecticut. Interviewer, Gary Y. Okihiro.
Ann Graybill Cook, June 10, 1994, State College, Pennsylvania. Interviewer, Gary Y. Okihiro.
Betty Emlen, June 9, 1994, Haverford, Pennsylvania. Interviewer, Gary Y. Okihiro.
Woodruff J. Emlen, June 9, 1994, Haverford, Pennsylvania. Interviewer, Gary Y. Okihiro.
Teruo Terry Hayashi, November 11, 1995, Pittsburgh, Pennsylvania. Interviewer, Gary Y. Okihiro.
Nobu Hibino, May 18, 1994, Portland, Connecticut. Interviewer, Gary Y. Okihiro.
Louise Seki Hoare, November 3, 1995, Santa Monica, California. Interviewer, Gary Y. Okihiro.
June S. Kawamura, November 4, 1995, Newport Beach, California. Interviewer, Gary Y. Okihiro.
Agnes Y. Kawate, November 3, 1995, Montebello, California. Interviewer, Gary Y. Okihiro.
Masako Amemiya MacFarlane, December 15, 1995, Los Gatos, California. Interviewer, Gary Y. Okihiro.
Alice Abe Matsumoto, April 12, 1996, Woodbury, Minnesota. Interviewer, Gary Y. Okihiro.
George Matsumoto, December 14, 1995, Oakland, California. Interviewer, Gary Y. Okihiro.
Yoshio Matsumoto, April 12, 1996, Woodbury, Minnesota. Interviewer, Gary Y. Okihiro.
Albert K. Mineta, December 15, 1995, San Jose, California. Interviewer, Gary Y. Okihiro.

Kenji Murase, August 26, 1995, San Francisco, California. Interviewer, Gary Y. Okihiro.

John W. Nason, June 9, 1994, Kennett Square, Pennsylvania. Interviewer, Gary Y. Okihiro.

Shunji F. Nishi, December 14, 1995, Berkeley, California. Interviewer, Gary Y. Okihiro.

Lafayette Noda, May 18, 1994, Portland, Connecticut. Interviewer, Gary Y. Okihiro.

Mary Otani, December 14, 1995, Richmond, California. Interviewer, Gary Y. Okihiro.

Margaret Cosgrave Sowers, December 11, 1993, Palo Alto, California. Interviewer, Gary Y. Okihiro.

William C. Stevenson, August 23, 1995, Berkeley, California. Interviewer, Gary Y. Okihiro.

Esther Torii Suzuki, April 11, 1996, Minneapolis, Minnesota. Interviewer, Gary Y. Okihiro.

Kayo Suzukida, November 18, 1995, Evanston, Illinois. Interviewer, Gary Y. Okihiro.

Nao Takasugi, November 20, 1993, Oxnard, California. Interviewer. Gary Y. Okihiro.

Maye M. Uemura, April 12, 1996, St. Paul, Minnesota. Interviewer, Gary Y. Okihiro.

Kay Yamashita, April 6, 1994, Chicago, Illinois. Interviewer, Gary Y. Okihiro.

Minoru Yoshida, April 13, 1996, Minneapolis, Minnesota. Interviewer, Gary Y. Okihiro.

Published and Unpublished Sources

Adamic, Louis. *From Many Lands.* New York: Harper & Brothers, 1939.

Aptheker, Herbert. *Anti-Racism in U.S. History: The First Two Hundred Years.* Westport, Connecticut: Praeger, 1993.

Barstow, Robbins W. "Help for 'Nisei' Students." *Christian Century* 59, no. 26 (July 1, 1942): 836–37.

Chan, Sucheng. *Asian Americans: An Interpretive History.* Boston: Twayne, 1991.

——. "Race, Ethnic Culture, and Gender in the Construction of Identities among Second-Generation Chinese Americans, 1880s to 1930s." In *Claiming America: Constructing Chinese American Identities During the Exclusion Era,* edited by K. Scott Wong and Sucheng Chan. Philadelphia: Temple University Press, 1998.

Chin, Frank, Jeffery Paul Chan, Lawson Fusao Inada, and Shawn Wong, eds. *Aiiieeeee! An Anthology of Asian-American Writers.* Garden City, N.Y.: Anchor Press, 1975.

The Log of Christopher Columbus. Translated by Robert H. Fuson. Camden, Maine: International Marine Publishing, 1987.

Commission on Wartime Relocation and Internment of Civilians. *Personal Justice Denied*. Washington, D.C.: Government Printing Office, 1982.

Cosgrave, Margaret. "Relocation of American-Japanese Students." *Journal of the American Association of Collegiate Registrars*, April 1943, pp. 221–26.

Cowles, LeRoy E. *University of Utah and World War II*. Salt Lake City: Deseret News Press, 1949.

Daniels, Roger. *Concentration Camps: North America, Japanese in the United States and Canada During World War II*. Malabar, Fla.: Robert E. Krieger Publishing, 1981.

——. *The Decision to Relocate the Japanese Americans*. Philadelphia: J. B. Lippincott, 1975.

——. *Prisoners Without Trial: Japanese Americans in World War II*. New York: Hill and Wang, 1993.

Drinnon, Richard. *Keeper of Concentration Camps: Dillon S. Myer and American Racism*. Berkeley: University of California Press, 1987.

Dublin, Murray. "Helped Long Ago, They Help Now." *Philadelphia Inquirer*, May 15, 1990.

Embree, John F. "Resistance to Freedom—An Administrative Problem." *Applied Anthropology* 2, no. 4 (September 1943): 10–14.

From Camp to College: The Story of Japanese American Student Relocation. Philadelphia: National Japanese American Student Relocation Council, n.d.

Girdner, Audrie, and Anne Loftis. *The Great Betrayal: The Evacuation of the Japanese-Americans During World War II*. London: Macmillan, 1969.

Grodzins, Morton. *Americans Betrayed: Politics and the Japanese Evacuation*. Chicago: University of Chicago Press, 1949.

Hale, William Q. "Japanese-American Student Evacuation and Relocation." Manuscript, Pendle Hill, Wallingford, Pennsylvania, 1943.

Hall, William W., Jr. *The Small College Talks Back: An Intimate Appraisal*. New York: Richard R. Smith, 1951.

Hayashi, Ann Koto. "Face of the Enemy, Heart of a Patriot: Japanese-American Internment Narratives." Ph.D. dissertation, Ohio State University, 1992.

——. *Face of the Enemy, Heart of a Patriot: Japanese-American Internment Narratives*. New York: Garland Publishing, 1995.

Hirano, Kiyo. *Enemy Alien*. San Francisco: JAM Publications, 1983.

Hosokawa, Bill. "A Good Man, A Good Cause." *Pacific Citizen*, December 4–11, 1992.

——. *Nisei: The Quiet Americans*. New York: William Morrow, 1969.

Ichioka, Yuji. *The Issei: The World of the First Generation Japanese Immigrants, 1885–1924*. New York: Free Press, 1988.

Ima, Kenji, and Ruben G. Rumbaut. "Southeast Asian Refugees in American Schools: A Comparison of Fluent-English-Proficient and Limited-English-Proficient Students." In *The Asian American Experience: A Source Book for Teachers and Students*, edited by Don T. Nakanishi and Tina Yamano Nishida. New York: Routledge, 1995.

Irons, Peter. *Justice At War.* New York: Oxford University Press, 1983.

Ito, Kazuo. *Issei: A History of Japanese Immigrants in North America.* Translated by Shinichiro Nakamura and Jean S. Gerard. Seattle: Japanese Community Service, 1973.

Ito, Leslie A. "Loyalty and Learning: Nisei Women and the Student Relocation." B.A. honors thesis, Mount Holyoke College, 1996.

James, Thomas. *Exile Within: The Schooling of Japanese Americans, 1942–1945.* Cambridge: Harvard University Press, 1987.

Kibria, Nazli. *Family Tightrope: The Changing Lives of Vietnamese Americans.* Princeton: Princeton University Press, 1993.

Kitagawa, Daisuke. *Issei and Nisei: The Internment Years.* New York: Seabury Press, 1967.

Kumamoto, Bob. "The Search for Spies: American Counterintelligence and the Japanese American Community, 1931–1942." *Amerasia Journal* 6, no. 2 (1979): 45–75.

Lind, Andrew W. *Hawaii's Japanese: An Experiment in Democracy.* Princeton: Princeton University Press, 1946.

Lukes, Timothy J., and Gary Y. Okihiro. *Japanese Legacy: Farming and Community Life in California's Santa Clara Valley.* Cupertino: California History Center, 1985.

McClain, Laurene Wu. "Donaldina Cameron: A Reappraisal." *Pacific Historian* 27, no. 3 (Fall 1983): 25–35.

Martin, Mildred Crowl. *Chinatown's Angry Angel: The Story of Donaldina Cameron.* Palo Alto, California: Pacific Books, 1977.

Marutani, Bill. "AFSC Remembered." *Pacific Citizen,* June 18, 1982.

Matsumoto, Alice Abe. "Memoirs." In *Reflections: Memoirs of Japanese American Women in Minnesota,* edited by John Nobuya Tsuchida. Covina, California: Pacific Asia Press, 1994.

Matsumoto, Toru. *Beyond Prejudice: A Story of the Church and Japanese Americans.* New York: Friendship Press, 1946.

Matsumoto, Valerie. "Japanese American Women During World War II." In *Unequal Sisters: A Multicultural Reader in U.S. Women's History,* edited by Ellen Carol DuBois and Vicki L. Ruiz. New York: Routledge, 1990.

Mezzacappa, Dale. "Survivors at the Head of the Class." *Philadelphia Inquirer,* June 14, 1990.

Montag, Guy. "The Grinnell Nisei." Manuscript, Grinnell College, May 17, 1984.

Murakami, Satoko. "I Am Alive." *Common Ground* 2:3 (Spring 1942): 15–18.

Myer, Dillon S. *Uprooted Americans: The Japanese Americans and the War Relocation Authority During World War II.* Tucson: University of Arizona Press, 1971.

Niiya, Brian, ed. *Japanese American History: An A-to-Z Reference from 1868 to the Present.* New York: Facts on File, 1993.

"Nisei: Disguised Blessing." *Newsweek,* December 29, 1958.

"Nisei Students in Junior College: A Symposium." *Junior College Journal* 14, no. 1 (September 1943): 5–11.

"Nisei Students Speak for Themselves: A Symposium." *Junior College Journal* 14, no. 6 (February 1944): 243–44.

O'Brien, Robert W. *The College Nisei.* Palo Alto, California: Pacific Books, 1949.

———. "Reaction of the College Nisei to Japan and Japanese Foreign Policy from the Invasion of Manchuria to Pearl Harbor." *Pacific Northwest Quarterly* 36, no. 1 (January 1945): 19–28.

———. "Student Relocation." *Common Ground* 3, no. 4 (Summer 1943): 73–78.

Okihiro, Gary Y. *Cane Fires: The Anti-Japanese Movement in Hawaii, 1865–1945.* Philadelphia: Temple University Press, 1991.

———. *Margins and Mainstreams: Asians in American History and Culture.* Seattle: University of Washington Press, 1994.

———. *Teaching Asian American History.* Washington, D.C.: American Historical Association, 1997.

Okihiro, Gary Y., and Julie Sly. "The Press, Japanese Americans, and the Concentration Camps." *Phylon* 44, no. 1 (March 1983): 66–83.

Osajima, Keith. "Asian Americans as the Model Minority: An Analysis of the Popular Press Image in the 1960s and 1980s." In *Reflections on Shattered Windows: Promises and Prospects for Asian American Studies,* edited by Gary Y. Okihiro et al. Pullman: Washington State University Press, 1988.

Pascoe, Peggy. *Relations of Rescue: The Search for Female Moral Authority in the American West, 1874–1939.* New York: Oxford University Press, 1990.

Petersen, William. *Japanese Americans: Oppression and Success.* New York: Random House, 1971.

Polenberg, Richard. "The Good War? A Reappraisal of How World War II Affected American Society." *Virginia Magazine of History and Biography* 100, no. 3 (July 1992): 295–322.

"The Problem of Student Nurses of Japanese Ancestry." *American Journal of Nursing* 43, no. 10 (October 1943): 895–96.

Provinse, John H. "Relocation of Japanese-American College Students: Acceptance of a Challenge." *Higher Education* 1, no. 8 (April 16, 1945): 1–4.

Richardson, O. D. "Nisei Evacuees—Their Challenge to Education." *Junior College Journal* 8, no. 1 (September 1942): 6–12.

Ryan, Barbara Haddad. "From Camps to Campus." *Swarthmore College Bulletin,* February 1993, 20–25.

Sarasohn, Eileen Sunada, ed. *The Issei: Portrait of a Pioneer.* Palo Alto: Pacific Books, 1983.

Smith, Henry Nash. *Virgin Land: The American West as Symbol and Myth.* Cambridge: Harvard University Press, 1950.

Smith, M. Joan. "Background, Problems and Significant Reactions of Relocated Japanese American Students." Ed.D. thesis, Syracuse University, 1949.

Stoddard, Lothrop. *The Rising Tide of Color Against White World-Supremacy.* New York: Charles Scribner's Sons, 1920.

"Success Story: Outwhiting the Whites." *Newsweek*, June 21, 1971.

Suzuki, Esther Torii. "Memoirs." In *Reflections: Memoirs of Japanese American Women in Minnesota*, edited by John Nobuya Tsuchida. Covina, Calif.: Pacific Asia Press, 1994.

Takaki, Ronald. *Pau Hana: Plantation Life and Labor in Hawaii, 1835–1920*. Honolulu: University of Hawaii Press, 1983.

———. *Strangers from a Different Shore: A History of Asian Americans*. Boston: Little, Brown, 1989.

Tamura, Eileen H. *Americanization, Acculturation, and Ethnic Identity: The Nisei Generation in Hawaii*. Urbana: University of Illinois Press, 1994.

Tateishi, John. *And Justice for All: An Oral History of the Japanese American Detention Camps*. New York: Random House, 1984.

Thuy, Vung G. "The Indochinese in America." In *The Education of Asian and Pacific Americans: Historical Perspectives and Prescriptions for the Future*, edited by Don T. Nakanishi and Marsha Hirano-Nakanishi. Phoenix: Onyx Press, 1983.

Turk, Barnett. "A Land-Locked World Away." *Alumni Voice* [University of Missouri–Kansas City], Summer 1987.

Uchida, Take. "An Issei Internee's Experiences." In *Japanese Americans: From Relocation to Redress*, rev. ed., edited by Roger Daniels, Sandra C. Taylor, Harry H. L. Kitano. Seattle: University of Washington Press, 1991.

Uemura, Maye Mitsuye Oye. "Memoirs." In *Reflections: Memoirs of Japanese American Women in Minnesota*, edited by John Nobuya Tsuchida. Covina, Calif.: Pacific Asia Press, 1994.

Villalva, Lydia. "12 Southeast Asian Students Awarded Scholarships." *St. Paul Pioneer Press Dispatch*, May 10, 1987.

Yamamoto, J. K. "Members of the Japanese American Student Relocation Council Honored." *Hokubei Mainichi*, April 22, 1995.

INDEX

175